2 in 1

BREAD MACHINECOOKBOOK

for Beginners & Next Level

From Basics to Advance Use:

Classic and Most Beloved Breads, Gourmet, Jams,

Snacks and More, All Homemade!

By

QUEENIE MALLIN

TABLE OF CONTENTS

CHAPTER 6: PROPER STORAGE AND PRESERVATION OF BREAD 21

BOOK 2: BREAD MACHINE COOKBOOK 22

CHAPTER 1: BASIC BREAD RECIPES 23

CHAPTER 2: SWEET & BREAKFAST BREAD RECIPES 33

CHAPTER 3: WHOLE BREAD RECIPES 43

CHAPTER 4: HOLIDAY BREAD RECIPES 53

CHAPTER 5: SPICE, HERB & VEGETABLE BREAD RECIPES 65

CHAPTER 6: CHEESE BREAD RECIPES 75

As a token of appreciation for choosing "Bread Machine Cookbook," we have a delightful surprise for you. Not one, but **TWO EXCLUSIVE BONUSES** await you.

Advanced Guide Bonus: Unlock the secrets of maximizing your bread machine's potential. This guide offers in-depth knowledge from advanced techniques to specialized recipes like vegan treats, lactose-free breads, delicious sauces, and so much more.

Special Surprise Bonus: Dive deeper into the advanced guide and discover an exclusive reward designed to fuel your culinary passion.

Curious about how to access these bonuses? Head over to the dedicated BONUS SECTION in this book to find out how to download and enjoy them.

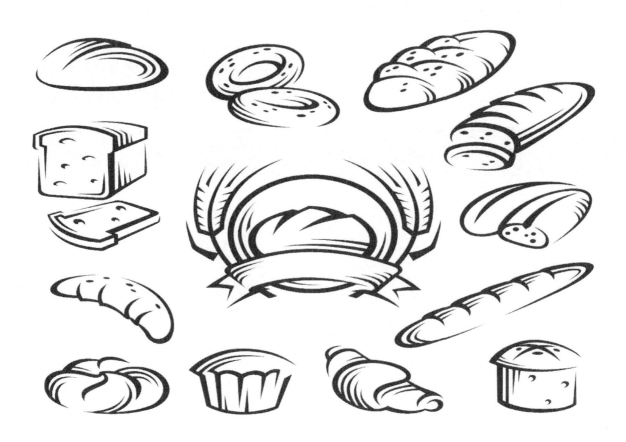

Homemade bread is both flavorful and nutritious, but its preparation often demands time and effort. However, with a bread machine, you can revel in the aroma and taste of freshly baked bread without investing much elbow grease.

Even though store-bought bread is easy to find, making your own at home has a number of benefits. You have the liberty to customize the bread to fit your family's dietary needs and flavor preferences. Using a bread machine, you can produce wonderful loaves using simple ingredients like flour, water, yeast, and salt.

What sets home-baked bread apart is the absence of artificial additives, often found in commercial bread. You have the freedom to enhance your bread with wholesome add-ins like grains or seeds.

One of the joys of baking at home is the control over ingredient quality and the ability to adapt it to your liking.

Also, making bread the old-fashioned way can leave you with a lot of things to clean. On the other hand, all you have to do with a bread machine is put in the ingredients and clean the pan after baking.

Modern bread machines offer an array of customization features, enabling users to produce a vast variety of breads. For those managing food sensitivities like gluten intolerance, a bread machine can be a game-changer.

This book offers an extensive collection of bread recipes. You need to use fresh ingredients, set your machine, and then forget about it, awaiting the delightful outcome.

For those who have never made bread before and have no idea where to begin, using a bread machine or bread maker is a godsend. With the help of a bread machine, they can now bake like professionals with consistently delicious results. Through its automatic programming, it can handle everything from mixing to kneading to shaping the dough. The digital appliance bakes bread at precisely the right quantity, time, and temperature. Because bread is a staple in so many diets, having a bread maker at home may be a huge time saver when planning meals. Bread machines always feature the bread pan inside for storing the dough and the paddles right at the bottom of the pan. The machine's permanent heating element provides uniform heat throughout the vessel.

1.1 Types of Bread Machines

There are many kinds of bread machines out there, but the most popular ones are:

1.1.1 Basic Bread Machines

These are straightforward versions meant to produce basic breads such as white or whole wheat. They often have fewer options and may lack features for preparing specialty breads.

1.1.2 Multi-Program Bread Machines

These machines have several pre-programmed settings that allow you to manufacture several sorts of bread. They can manage gluten-free, artisan, sweet bread, French bread, and other recipes.

1.1.3 Convection Bread Machines

In a convection bread machine, a convection fan moves hot air around the baking area. This function encourages even bread baking and browning, resulting in a more consistent and professional-looking loaf.

1.2 Cycles and Settings

A bread machine can be used in a variety of ways. Majority of bread machines include settings for the mixing, the kneading, the resting, the rising, the punching, and the baking in the following cycles: basic bread, French bread, rapid bake, sweet bread, gluten-free, whole-wheat bread, cake, and jam.

1.2.1 Bread Machine Cycles

Bread machines run through cycles that involve the following:

1. Kneading

The first stage, kneading, entails a thorough mixing of the ingredients. Time ranges from 15 minutes to 45 minutes, based on machine strength and bread kind.

2. Rest

The dough is allowed to rest (or "autolyze" in baking terminology) between rounds of kneading. The dough and the gluten in it need time to rest so that they can absorb the surrounding moisture. Bread makers vary in how long the "rest" cycle lasts (between 5 and 35 minutes), as does the type of bread being made.

3. Rise

During this phase, the dough rises, creating an airy and light loaf. The "rise" occurs when the temperature of the dough is raised to between 75- and 80-degrees Fahrenheit, at which point the yeast can ferment in around 40 to 50 minutes. The cycle time may go up depending on what kind of bread is being made. French bread, for instance, needs at least 60+ minutes to complete.

4. Punch

In the "punch" cycle, the dough is kneaded once again, although this time with much less force. The purpose of punching the bread dough is primarily to eliminate trapped gas from the previous cycle's yeast fermentation. It's the shortest possible cycle, clocking in at under a minute.

5. Bake

The baking is done during this cycle. Based on the type of bread and model of the bread machine, it can take anywhere from 30 minutes to 90 minutes.

The type of bread being created and the kind of bread machine determine which cycles are used in conjunction with one another by the bread machine. Some types of bread, such as French bread, require more time for rising and kneading than gluten-free bread.

1.2.2 Bread Machine Settings

The bread machine may be used in a variety of ways, and there are several different settings to choose from.

1. Basic Bread

The Basic Bread can be utilized to make a variety of breads, including regular white, potato, garlic, and the other savory varieties. It is among the most common cycle combination, lasting three to four hours.

2. Sweet Bread

This three-hour option includes sweet components such as sugar, cinnamon, sweet nuts, dried fruits, and others. The Sweet Bread cycle is similar to the Basic Bread cycle; however, it has the lower temperature of 65 to 70 degrees Fahrenheit.

3. Whole-Wheat Cycle

This is ideal for baking the doughs that have a high percentage of gluten, whole wheat, or cracked grain and require extra time for rising and kneading correctly.

4. French Bread

This cycle is appropriate for making thicker crusts, such as sourdough, and requires more time for kneading, rising, and baking, typically taking four hours.

5. Gluten-Free Bread

This setting speeds up the bread-making process compared to the other four cycles (sweet bread, basic bread, whole-wheat bread, and French bread). Because gluten is not present, less time is needed for knead, rest, and rise. Creating gluten-free bread takes about two hours.

6. Rapid Bake

This setting allows the bread to bake in 60 to 90 minutes, which is much less time than the other settings.

7. Cake and Jam

You can use this cycle for making your choice of jams, preserves, compotes, and other sweet sort of delicacies like cakes! Jam takes 55 minutes to prepare, while cakes and the other delicacies take 80 minutes.

1.3 Common Features

Most bread machines include typical features that make the bread-making process easier:

1.3.1 Loaf Size Selection

Depending on your needs, select a loaf size ranging from 1 lb. to 2.5 lbs.

1.3.2 Crust Color Selection

To modify the appearance and flavor of the crust, choose a crust color such as light, medium, or dark.

1.3.3 Delay Timer

Allows you to specify a time delay for the baking process to begin later, so you can enjoy freshly made bread when you wake up or get home from work.

1.3.4 Keep Warm Option

This feature keeps the bread warm after baking for a set period of time, ensuring that your bread stays fresh until you're ready to consume it.

1.3.5 Preheat Option

Some advanced models include a preheat function to guarantee that the ingredients are at the proper temperature before the baking cycle begins.

1.4 How Does a Bread Machine Work?

Making tasty homemade bread with a bread machine is a simple and user-friendly process that requires little effort. Here are the fundamentals of using a bread machine:

1.4.1 Learn About Your Machine

Read the instruction booklet and experiment with the many features of the model you've chosen, such as delayed baking, different cycle kinds, and loaf length. You might have to try out different recipes and products before you find the right mix.

Some machines have memory setting cards that you can either write on or leave blank for your notes. Filling one of these cards with a bread recipe allows you to remember the settings or put a message to remind yourself of what worked for you.

1.4.2 Prepare the Ingredients

Choose the kind of bread you wish to make. If you are confused about how much flour or additional ingredients to use, consult the handbook or recipe book. Most machines have a measuring container that can carry either flour or liquids; you can use this instead of measuring by hand. Add the ingredients inside the bread machine as per the manufacturer's directions.

1.4.3 Place the bread pan and ingredients in the machine.

Some bread machines include either a removable or non-removable bread pan. Ensure that the ingredients are added to the pan in the proper sequence.

1.4.4 Choose Your Settings

Choose your favorite cycle. If your chosen cycle does not come with a pre-programmed set time, you must set your own. Your instructions and recipe book should guide you. The timer displays the total time required to bake, including the waiting period. Select the timer for desired time you want the bread to bake. Set it for when you want to start cooking. For instance, it's 9 p.m., and you want to go to bed, but you want the bread to be done by 7 a.m. So you'll set your timer for 10 hours. To start the countdown, press the start button.

1.4.5 Start the Machine

Having the machine ready and programmed before going to bed will help you obtain a better night's sleep. Some systems may also let you program a delayed start, which might be useful if you are not going to be home when the bread first emerges.

1.4.6 Begin Cooking

After you've made your selections, press the start button. Nothing appears to happen after pressing the start button on a bread machine that waits for the ingredients to reach the proper temperature. In general, it should begin its cycle within the next hour.

If your bread maker has a removable kneading blade, remember to remove it before the baking cycle begins. What you don't want is for it to sink to the bottom of the loaf while baking.do you? If you fail to remove it, you'll notice an unsightly hole in the finished product when you do.

While it may be tempting to peek, do not do so because it may change the temperature inside the bread machine. However, if your machine has a viewing window, you can peek in and observe how your bread dough is shaping. If you choose to add fruits, spices, raisins, or nuts, the machine will sound an alarm to let you know when to do so.

A large white loaf takes 3-4 hours to bake on average, while whole grain bread takes 4 hours or more. Using the rapid-bake setting on your bread machine will allow you to bake for around an hour. The longer you bake with the rapid bake setting, the better the results.

1.4.7 Examine the Bread

If your bread is done after the cycle is complete, carefully lift the lid (it may be hot, so put on oven mitts to avoid burning your fingers) and remove the bread.

1.4.8 Take out the Bread

As the bread is baked, take it out right away and do not leave it in the machine. This will prevent overcooking and preserve the bread's texture and color. Let it cool on a cooling rack for about half an hour before slicing it. The purpose of cooling is to allow the water molecules to escape so that the inside of the loaf is moist rather than spongy.

1.5 Cleaning and Maintenance

Cleaning and maintaining your bread machine properly is critical to ensuring its longevity and best performance.

1.5.1 Unplug the Machine

To minimize accidents, always disconnect the bread machine before cleaning it.

1.5.2 Remove the Bread Residue

Remove the bread pan and kneading paddles after each usage to clean them. To clean these areas, use warm soapy water and a gentle sponge or brush.

1.5.3 Wipe Down the Interior and Exterior

Wipe the interior and exterior of the machine down with a moist cloth. Avoid using abrasive materials that could damage the surface.

1.5.4 Clean the Lid and Control Panel

Wipe the lid and control panel with a moist cloth, being careful not to let water inside the machine.

1.5.5 Regular Maintenance

For detailed maintenance requirements, such as lubricating moving parts or cleaning air vents, consult your machine's user handbook.

1.5.6 Storage

When not in use, keep the bread machine in a cool, dry location and keep it clean and clear of residue.

By following these simple procedures, you can bake wonderful homemade bread in your bread machine and keep it in good shape for years to come.

Remember to always refer to the user manual for your specific bread machine for complete instructions and safety guidelines, as different models may have unique features and requirements. Happy baking!

Basic bread making requires simple ingredients: flour, yeast, salt, and liquid. Sugar, fats, and eggs are some of the other elements that contribute flavor, texture, and nutrition to bread. The following are the essential ingredients:

2.1 Flour

Flour is the starting point for baking bread. The quality of bread is determined by the quality of the flour. When blended with different components and in different settings, each variety of flour behaves differently. This is why it is critical to always use the flour specified in the recipe. Wheat flour is the most widely in bread machine. Wheat flour comes in an array of varieties, including all-purpose, whole wheat & bread flour. Bread flour is more powerful than other wheat flour. It can also survive the bread maker's activities better than the others. Bread flour also has a higher protein concentration, which aids in the development of gluten. It is important to note that bread flour contains more gluten than all-purpose flour. This makes it ideal for bread loaves, as it adds height to the loaf.

Other grains' flours, such as rice, rye, corn, buckwheat, or oat, can also be used in various bread recipes. However, make sure the flour is as fresh as possible. If you have the time, you could do it yourself. Loaves of bread made with home-milled flours are typically lighter and moister. When purchasing whole wheat flour, exercise caution. Some of the store varieties have been treated to remove oils. The things for sale may or may not be made entirely of wheat flour.

Do not pack the flour into the measuring cup; instead, spoon the flour you are using and level with a flat spoon. Using the measuring cup as a scoop will result in more flour than required in the recipe. When too much flour is utilized in a recipe, the result is hard and dense produce. Store flour in moisture-proof, airtight containers to extend its shelf life, keep it dry and fresh, and keep bugs out.

2.2 Fats

The most frequent fats used in bread preparation are butter, oil, and margarine. Fats add taste, lubricate the dough, and improve bread quality, keeping the crumb soft. It also keeps the bread fresher for longer (by a day or two). Bread dough can be made with almost any fat, such as lard, peanut oil, or olive oil. One fat can be swapped for another. For example, if the recipe calls for 1 cup of butter, you can substitute any other cup of your preferred fat.

If you don't want to use any fat but want the benefits it brings to your baked bread, try prune butter, apple butter, or applesauce. These will work perfectly! Before using, slice the butter or margarine into little pats so that it will integrate nicely with added components.

2.3 Yeast

There are several types of dry yeast on the market. Active dry yeast, bread machine yeast, rapid-rise yeast, and instant yeast are examples of these. Fresh yeast is vital for successful bread-making. It is, therefore, critical to double-check the "Best if used by" date on the package before purchasing. If you are unclear about which yeast to buy, choose one that is labeled "active dry" or buy yeast that says on the jar that it is designed for bread-making machines. Store-bought yeast packets typically contain 2 1/4 cups of active dry yeast. When creating bread in a bread machine, one packet can usually replace two teaspoons of yeast.

Unopened dry yeast should not be refrigerated or frozen. Simply keep it in a dark & cool location. Refrigerate for up to 120 days after opening or freeze for up to 6 months. For express or rapid bake bread machine cycles, do not use active dry yeast. For regular cycle bread machines, use 1/2 teaspoon of instant yeast per 1 cup of flour in your recipe. However, if utilizing rapid or express bread machine cycles (which take less than 2 hours to process bread), double or triple the yeast amount. Each machine has its own recommended liquid temperature; make sure to follow your manufacturer's directions.

All forms of dry yeast are OK for use in recipes. Bread machine yeast is 50 percent faster than regular yeast. Instant yeast is also stronger than other varieties and faster-acting, making it ideal for use in bread makers. Rapid-rise yeast should not be used because it is not ideal for bread machines. It rises too quickly, not allowing the dough to develop its flavor. You may only use it if you are in a hurry or if your bread machine has a rapid-bake cycle.

Avoid putting the yeast in direct contact with sugar or salt. This will inhibit yeast activity. Make a small indentation in the flour with the back of a spoon and sprinkle the yeast into the center. This will prevent the yeast from coming into contact with the liquid until the cycle begins.

2.4 Eggs

In many bread recipes, eggs are used to add moisture, color, and flavor. It's important to use large eggs in your recipes unless the recipe calls for a different size. When you use eggs in a bread machine, they should be at room temperature. Cold eggs might not mix as effectively with other ingredients. If you forget to take them out of the refrigerator ahead of time, simply put them in a container of warm water for a few minutes to bring them to a normal temperature.

2.5 Salt

Salt is an essential ingredient in bread recipes. It regulates the rising process and enriches the flavor of your bread. If you're worried about the amount of salt in your diet, it can be reduced by half. However, eliminating it entirely may result in bland bread.

2.6 Sugar

Sugar acts as food for the yeast, allowing it to become active and start the fermentation process. It also enhances the flavor, crust color, and texture of the bread. Add a pinch or the recommended amount of sugar. Sugar can also be substituted with honey, molasses, or corn syrup. However, this will change the flavor of your bread.

2.7 Liquid

Water or milk is the most commonly used liquid in bread recipes. Liquid activates the yeast, binds the ingredients together, and helps in the dough's gluten development. Milk is used in recipes to add flavor and produce a fine crumb. Milk also improves the keeping quality of bread and produces a softer crust than water. The milk must be heated to approximately 80°F (27°C) before it is combined with other ingredients. Cold liquids can potentially inhibit the yeast's activity.

While bread machines simplify the task of making bread, the basic principles of baking remain the same. The application of these concepts to a bread machine is as follows:

3.1 Ingredients

As in traditional bread making, you will need the same ingredients in the bread machine: yeast, flour, water, salt, and sweeteners/fats. Measure them accurately according to your machine's instructions.

3.2 Scaling Ingredients

Accurate ingredient measurement is critical for consistent results in bread baking. Accurate measuring guarantees that the flour, water, yeast, salt, and other components are proportioned properly.

3.3 Kneading

Automatic Kneading: A paddle or kneading hook built into bread machines mixes and kneads the dough. The machine's motor-driven kneading mimics the manual process of gluten development.

3.4 Fermentation (Proofing)

Bread machines have a rising cycle where the dough rests and ferments. The machine generates a controlled warmed atmosphere to enhance yeast activity and dough growth.

3.5 Scoring and Shaping

Automated Shaping: Bread machines manage shaping automatically. You add the ingredients, and the machine does the kneading and rising. However, if you want a certain shape, you can use the dough cycle, remove the dough, shape it by hand, and then return it to the baking.

3.6 Baking

Baking Cycle Precision: A baking cycle in bread machines ensures that the dough is baked to perfection. This automated baking method keeps time and temperature settings accurate.

3.7 Cooling

Controlled Cooling: Bread machines frequently feature a cooling phase after baking to slowly reduce the temperature of the loaf, producing a good texture and preventing moisture accumulation.

3.8 Experimentation and Observation

Although it is not possible to physically examine the progress of the dough as is the case with traditional methods, listening to the sounds and patterns of the machine can provide useful insights into the firing steps.

3.9 Recipe Modification

Recipe adaptation is essential, especially because bread machine performance varies. Consistent outcomes can be achieved by fine-tuning ingredient proportions or cycle selections.

3.10 Customization and Experimentation

Possibilities for Customization: Some modern bread machines have settings that can be customized. This allows you to experiment with kneading times, rising times, and even ingredient additions.

Understanding these essential principles and how they interact with bread machine operation will give you the confidence to make wonderful handmade bread. While bread machines make the process easier, understanding the underlying principles allows you to troubleshoot, adapt, and innovate to attain the desired results. Always refer to the manual for your individual bread machine for detailed instructions adapted to its characteristics.

CHAPTER 4: HOW TO ADAPT RECIPES FOR DIFFERENT SIZES

4.1 How to Measure Ingredients for Bread

Bread machines may have labels for 1, 1.5, or 2-lb loaves. This refers to the "flour capacity." To determine the flour capacity of any specific bread machine, consult the manufacturer's guide. If the manufacturer's manual regularly recommends 3-4 cups of flour, this is your bread machine's capacity. You can now convert oven recipes to bread machine recipes. Here are the general flour capacities for specific bread loaf weights:

- A 1-pound loaf from a bread machine requires 2 to 2-3/4 cups of flour.
- For a 1.5-pound loaf, use 3 to 4 cups of flour in a bread machine.
- For a 2-pound loaf, a bread machine will need between 4.5 and 5.5 cups of flour.

Table: Ingredient Proportions Based on Loaf Size

Ingredient	1-lb Loaf	1.5-lb Loaf	2-lb Loaf
Flour	2 - 2¾ cups	3 - 4 cups	4.5 - 5.5 cups
Yeast	Specific to recipe	1 tsp	1¼ tsp
Water	Adjust based on flour	Adjust based on flour	Adjust based on flour

When adapting oven recipes for the bread machine, consider the following:

- For a machine that produces a 1.5-pound loaf, use 1 teaspoon of yeast.
- For a 2-pound loaf, use 1 1/4 teaspoons.

- For a 1.5-pound bread machine, use three cups of flour; for a 2-pound one, use 4 cups.
- Adjust all other ingredients proportionally, including flour and yeast.
- If a recipe uses multiple flour types, sum the amounts and adjust accordingly. Total flour might range from 3 to 4 cups based on loaf size.
- In a bread machine, mix 1-3 tablespoons of gluten flour with all-purpose flour or simply use bread flour. For rye flour, combine it with one tablespoon of gluten flour if the main flour is bread flour.
- All the ingredients should be at room temperature and should be added in the order that the maker suggests.
- Include nuts, raisins, or dried fruits as listed or per the manufacturer's guidelines.
- For dough cycles, handle the dough with extra flour outside the machine for better manageability.
- Use a bread machine's whole-grain cycle for whole-wheat, rye, or other grain flours when available.
- Record the recipe and any modifications for future use.
- For rich and sweet breads, select the sweet bread cycle with a light crust.

4.2 Converting Recipes for Different Loaf Sizes

Adapting bread recipes for various loaf sizes ensures consistency and ideal texture. Here's how to adjust recipes for 1, 1.5 & 2 lbs. loaves, whether using a bread machine or traditional methods:

4.2.1 Proportions of Ingredients

Maintain standard ratios for key ingredients like flour, yeast, water, and salt. Increase amounts for larger loaves and decrease for smaller ones.

4.2.2 Ingredient Variations

- Flour: Adjust according to desired loaf size, increasing for larger and decreasing for smaller loaves.
- Yeast: Typically, doesn't need major adjustment. A satisfactory rise in a 1 lb. loaf will likely be effective for larger loaves.
- Water: Adapt based on flour changes. Bigger loaves might need more water.
- Sweeteners, Salt, Fats: Tweak based on taste, but significant changes due to size are rare.

4.2.3 Kneading and Rising

- Kneading Time: Larger loaves may need more kneading for gluten formation.
- Rising Time: Due to greater dough bulk, larger loaves might require extended rising times.

4.2.4 Shaping and Proofing

- Shaping: Modify the dough shape according to loaf size.
- Proofing Time: Larger loaves might need more time to rise, but look for visual signs like doubling in size.

4.2.5 Baking

- Baking Time: Adjust based on loaf size, with larger loaves requiring more time.
- Internal Temperature: Ensure it reaches about 190-200°F (88-93°C) for a properly baked loaf.
-

4.2.6 Experiment

Begin with minor adjustments, expecting some trial and error. Document modifications and outcomes to refine your recipe over time.

4.2.7 Bread Machines

Always refer to the machine's manual for specific guidance on adapting recipes for different loaf sizes. Some devices might offer preset options for this purpose.

Adjusting bread recipes for your preferred loaf sizes can personalize your bread-making experience. While initial attempts might require fine-tuning, your dedication will yield loaves tailored to your preferences. Always note and document modifications to continuously achieve optimal results

Bread baking is both an art and a science, and ingredient substitutions can be especially helpful when working with limited ingredients or dietary requirements. The goal of this list of popular ingredient substitutes is to offer you the opportunity to experiment. Instead of running to the shop or opting to utilize an alternative ingredient, you should be able to make adjustments without compromising the dish. Although the final appearance, flavor, and texture may differ, combining these suggestions with your own instincts and taste senses may result in something more delicious than the original recipe. Here's a complete guide on navigating ingredient substitutions while baking bread:

5.1 Flour

Why Substitute Flour? The flavor, feel, and nutritional content of your bread can all be significantly influenced by the flour. Your baking abilities may be improved if you know how to use various flours.

All-Purpose Flour: To enhance taste and nutrients, substitute with whole wheat flour, bread flour, or a combination of the two.

- **Gluten-Free Flour:** Choose gluten-free flour blends like rice flour, almond flour, or a ready-made gluten-free flour mix. Consider using xanthan gum to improve the texture.

5.2 Sugar

- White Sugar: Replace white sugar with brown sugar, maple syrup, honey, or coconut sugar. If necessary, adjust the liquid levels.

5.3 Butter/Oil

- Unsalted butter: Substitute with vegetable, olive, or coconut oil. Coconut oil can provide a delicate taste.

- Dairy-Free: For dairy-free options, use plant-based oils or vegan butter.

5.4 Eggs (Binding)

- Binding: Use mashed bananas, unsweetened applesauce, silken tofu, yogurt, or commercial egg substitutes for binding.

5.5 Milk

- Dairy Milk: Substitute any plant-based milk, including coconut, oat, almond, or soy milk.
- Buttermilk: To simulate the acidity of buttermilk, combine nondairy milk with vinegar or lemon juice.

5.6 Yeast

- Active Dry Yeast: Instant yeast can often be used interchangeably with active dry yeast. Follow the packaging instructions to adjust the amount slightly.

5.7 Salt

- Table Salt: Use kosher or sea salt, modifying the amount dependent on the coarseness of the salt.

5.8 Add-ins

- Seeds and nuts: Customize by adding your favorite nuts or seeds or omit them if allergies are a concern.
- Dried Fruits: Replace with fresh fruits in small bits or swap one type for another.

5.9 Gluten-Free Substitutes

- Xanthan Gum: Aids in the replication of gluten's binding properties in gluten-free recipes.
- Guar Gum: It is used as a binder in gluten-free recipes, it helps improve the texture and shelf life of baked goods.

5.10 Sweeteners

- Honey/Molasses: Replace with maple syrup, agave nectar, or a mixture of sweeteners.

5.11 Herbs and Spices

Note: If using fresh herbs instead of dried, increase the amount by about three times for a similar taste intensity.

- Tarragon: Chervil. Alternatively, double the basil amount.
- Thyme: Basil, marjoram, oregano, or rosemary are all options.
- Paprika: Chili powder.
- Parsley: Basil, chervil, or celery leaf are options.
- Rosemary: Thyme.
- Nutmeg, ground: Mace, allspice, or pumpkin pie spice are options. Alternatively, use half as much ground cinnamon or clove.
- Oregano: Basil or thyme.

5.12 Dairy Alternatives

- Cheese: Explore dairy-free substitutes made from nuts, soy, or vegetables.
- Yogurt: Choose nondairy yogurts such as coconut or almond milk yogurt.

5.13 Flavored Extracts

- Vanilla Extract: For a variety of flavors, try substituting with almond, coconut, or citrus extracts.

5.14 Vinegar

- White Vinegar: For acidity in recipes, substitute with apple cider vinegar or lemon juice.

5.15 Water alteration

Hydration Levels: Different flours absorb water at varying rates. To obtain the proper dough consistency, the water content must be adjusted. For example, whole wheat flours typically absorb more water than all-purpose flours. When switching between these types, increase the water content incrementally and monitor the dough's texture.

Keep note of your substitutions and their consequences because even small adjustments can have a big impact. You'll get a sense of which substitutions work best over time for your desired bread outcomes. Always keep any allergies or dietary limitations in mind when choosing alternatives.

CHAPTER 6: PROPER STORAGE AND PRESERVATION OF BREAD

Preserving Your Bread Machine Output: Once you've baked with your bread machine, figuring out how to store the extra loaves or portions is crucial. Considering the superior quality of machine-made bread, there's often more than what gets eaten at once. So, here are the best practices for storing what you make:

6.1 About Dough

Chilling:

Post-kneading, take the dough out of the machine. Intending to use it in the next three days? Cool it down in the fridge. Flatten it into a disc shape, either tuck it in a zip-lock bag or rest it in a lightly oiled container, shielded with cling film. Keep in mind that the fridge won't halt yeast activity. Hence, deflate the dough each day till it's thoroughly cold. When you're set to bake, shape the dough, let it puff up, and then cook.

Freezing:

Should you not utilize the dough in three days, freezing becomes essential due to the absence of preservatives in machine-made dough. Feel free to keep it frozen for a month. For usage, shift the dough from the freezer to the fridge for an overnight cooling, then mold, allow to rise, and bake. For ease, mold the dough into your desired shapes like braids or loaves before you cool or freeze. At baking o'clock, just unpack, let it get to room temperature, and cook.

6.2 For Baked Bread

6.2.1 Freezing Your Bread:

If you're keen on lengthening your loaf's shelf life, freezing comes in handy. Store it securely in a freezer-friendly pouch, be it the full loaf or just parts. For those who've frozen the complete bread, thawing in the fridge overnight is the go-to, ensuring the texture stays right, and it's set for even toasting. And don't forget to strip off the freezing wrap prior to defrosting. Short on time? Directly toast the slices or reheat the loaf in your oven at 325°F for roughly half an hour.

6.2.2 The Bread Storage Debate: Paper or Plastic?

A newly baked loaf stays prime for approximately three days. If your consumption falls within that, keep it in a paper pouch on your tabletop. Plastic pouches, though handy, speed up mold formation, making your bread stale quickly.

6.2.3 The Charm of Bread Boxes:

Bread boxes are a blend of utility and beauty for any culinary space. Such boxes ensure minimal air movement, shielding the bread from getting old. If sealing it is your aim but bugs worry you, tuck in an extra bread slice with your main loaf. This acts as a moisture magnet, helping maintain the right humidity.

6.2.4 Picking the Right Spot for Bread:

Where you store the bread makes a difference. Refrigeration might lead to quicker drying for bread in paper and faster molding for those in plastic because of inconsistent temps and the fridge's natural humidity control. Likewise, proximity to a dishwasher is a no-no due to its inherent warmth and dampness. Bread's best kept in a non-humid, cool nook, perhaps a deep kitchen drawer or shelf.

6.2.5 Opt for Reusable Bread Pouches:

In your journey to a greener lifestyle, reusable bread pouches are worth considering. They're gaining traction in the marketplace, many being machine-friendly and suited for freezing. Carry them for shopping, and directly slip in your fresh loaves. They're not just eco-conscious but also a solution to the crumb mess that ripped paper pouches leave behind. Crafted from air-permeable fabrics, these bags mirror the eco-efficient attributes of paper ones.

CHAPTER 1: BASIC BREAD RECIPES

1.1. Bread Machine Basic Bread

PREP.: 15 MINUTES | COOK: 2 HOURS 20 MIN.

SERVING: 1 LB. – 8 SLICES|1.5 LBS.- 12 SLICES| 2 LBS. – 16 SLICES.

N.F. (PER SERVING): CALORIES: ~260 | TOTAL FAT: ~3.5G |PROTEIN: ~7.5G | CARBS: ~48G

Ingredient	1 Lb.	1.5 Lbs.	2 Lbs.
o Lukewarm Water	2/3 cup	1 cup	1 1/4 cups
o Salt	½ teaspoon	1 teaspoon	1 ½ teaspoon
o Lukewarm Milk	¼ cup	1/3 cup	½ cup
o Sugar	1 1/2 tablespoons	3 tablespoons	1/4 cup
o Butter	2 tablespoons	3 tablespoons	¼ cup
o Unbleached All-Purpose Flour	1 2/3 cup	2 ½ cups	3 ¾ cups
o Yeast (instant dry yeast)	1 teaspoon	1 ½ teaspoons	2 teaspoons

Directions:

- Follow the manufacturer's recommended order and add every ingredients to the bread machine basket.
- Set the parameters for the basic white bread machine and start it up.
- Take the bread pan out when it is done baking.
- After about 5 minutes, jiggle the pan slightly to loosen the loaf, then transfer it to a rack to cool.

1.2. Traditional White Bread

PREP: 10 MINS | COOK: 3H 20M

SERVING: 1 LB. - 8 SLICES|1.5 LBS.- 812SLICES| 2 LBS. - 16 SLICES.

NF PER 1 LB. RECIPE: CAL: ~275 | FAT: ~3.5G | PROT: ~8G | CARBS: ~55G

Ingredient	1 Lb.	1.5 Lbs.	2 Lbs.
o *Lukewarm Water (110°F/45°C)*	2/3 cup	1 cup	1 1/4 cups
o *Salt*	1 teaspoon	1 1/2 teaspoons	2 teaspoons
o *Sugar*	2 tablespoons	3 tablespoons	4 tablespoons
o *Vegetable Oil*	2 tablespoons	3 tablespoons	4 tablespoons
o *Bread Flour*	2 cups	3 cups	4 cups
o *Yeast*	1 1/2 teaspoons	2 1/4 teaspoons	3 teaspoons

Directions:

- Follow the manufacturer's recommended order and add all the ingredients inside the bread machine (liquids first and then the dry).
- Select "White Bread" and select "Start."
- After baking, let it cool on the wire rack before cutting it.

Note: The order in which ingredients are added may vary depending on the brand of your bread machine. Consult your manual for specific recommendations. Always use oven mitts or mitts when removing hot bread from the machine to prevent possible burns.

PREP TIME: 30 MIN | COOK TIME: 2H 20M

SERVING: 1 LB. - 8SLICES|1.5 LBS.- 12SLICES| 2 LBS. - 16 SLICES.

N.F (PER 1 LB.): CALORIES 549.4 | FAT 9.1G | PROTEIN 18.2G | CARBS 40.9G

Ingredient	1 Lb.	1.5 Lbs.	2 Lbs.
o *Warm Water*	1 cup	1 1/4 cups	1 1/3 cups
o *Olive Oil*	1 tablespoon	1 1/4 tablespoons	1 1/2 tablespoons
o *Salt*	3/4 teaspoon	1 teaspoon	1 1/2 teaspoons
o *Sugar*	1 tablespoon	1 1/4 tablespoons	1 1/2 tablespoons
o *All-Purpose Flour or Bread Flour*	3 cups	3 3/4 cups	4 cups
o *Yeast*	1 1/4 teaspoons	1 1/2 teaspoons	2 teaspoons

Directions:

- First, add the warm water to your bread machine.
- Now, add the olive oil, salt, and sugar. After that, add the flour, ensuring the liquid ingredients are covered.
- Make a small hole in the middle of the flour. Make sure no liquid enters the hole. Put the yeast in the hole.
- Set the bread machine to the French Bread Cycle.
- After 5 minutes check on the dough. If you feel the dough is dry & hard then add 1/2 to 1 tablespoon of water until it becomes soft enough to roll into a ball.
- If the dough is wet, add a little flour & keep adding until it is the right consistency.
- When the bread is done baking, let it cool for about 10 minutes before cutting it.

PREP TIME: 10 MIN | COOK TIME: 3H

SERVING: 1 LB. - 6 SLICES|1.5 LBS.- 8 SLICES| 2 LBS. - 10 SLICES.

PER SERVING: CALORIES 320 | FAT 9G | PROTEIN 6G | CARBS 11G

Ingredient	1 Lb.	1.5 Lbs.	2 Lbs.
o Warm Water (45°C)	2/3 cup	1 cup	1 1/3 cups
o White Sugar	1 1/3 tablespoons	2 tablespoons	2 2/3 tablespoons
o Yeast	1 1/8 teaspoons	1 1/2 teaspoons	2 teaspoons
o Olive Oil	1 1/3 tablespoons	1/4 cup	1/3 cup
o Bread Flour	1 1/2 cups	3 cups	4 cups
o Salt	3/4 teaspoon	1 1/2 teaspoons	2 teaspoons

Directions:

- Mix the water, sugar, and yeast together in the pan of the bread machine.
- After dissolving the yeast, foam for 10 minutes.
- Add the olive oil to the mixture.
- Combine the yeast, sugar, flour, and salt.
- Select Basic Settings and then select the Start button. It takes three hours to finish the whole cycle.
- Wait about 8-10 minutes before slicing the bread.

PREP.: 25 MINUTES | COOK: 2 TO 3 HOURS

SERVING: 1 LB. - 6 SLICES | 1.5 LBS.- 8 SLICES | 2 LBS. - 10 SLICES.

PER SERVING: CALORIES 131 | TOTAL FAT 2G | PROTEIN 4G | CARBS 24G

Ingredient	1 Lb.	1.5 Lbs.	2 Lbs.
o Buttermilk (80°F)	1/2 cup	2/3 cup	3/4 cup
o Melted and Cooled Butter	3/4 teaspoon	1 tablespoon	1 1/4 teaspoons
o Sugar	3/4 teaspoon	1 tablespoon	1 1/4 teaspoons
o Salt	1/2 teaspoon	3/4 teaspoon	1 teaspoon
o Baking Powder	1/3 teaspoon	1/4 teaspoon	1/2 teaspoon
o White Bread Flour	1 1/3 cups	1 3/4 cups	2 1/4 cups
o Instant Yeast	3/4 teaspoon	1 1/8 teaspoons	1 1/2 teaspoons

Directions:

- Add all ingredients to the basket of the machine by following the manufacturer's order.
- Set the machine's program to Basic or White Bread and the Medium type of crust.
- START the program.
- Let the cycle run completely.
- When the bread is done, take it out of the basket and leave it for five minutes to cool.
- Shake the bucket gently to dislodge the loaves.
- Place on a cooling rack to cool then slice and serve.

PREP.: 25 MINUTES | COOK: 3½ HOURS

SERVING: 1 LB. - 6 SLICES|1.5 LBS.- 8 SLICES| 2 LBS. - 10 SLICES.

PER SERVING: CALORIES 302 | TOTAL FAT 10G | PROTEIN 7G | CARBS 45G

Ingredient	1 Lb.	1.5 Lbs.	2 Lbs.
o Water	3/4 cup	1 cup	1 1/4 cups
o Salt	3/4 teaspoon	1 teaspoon	1 1/4 teaspoons
o Butter	2 teaspoons	2 1/2 tablespoons	2 1/2 tablespoons
o Sugar	1 1/2 teaspoons	2 1/2 teaspoons	2 1/2 teaspoons
o Flour	1 1/2 cups	2 1/4 cups	3 cups
o Semolina	1/4 cup	1/3 cup	1/3 cup
o Dry Yeast	1 teaspoon	1 1/2 teaspoons	2 teaspoons

Directions:

- Add all ingredients to the basket of the machine by following the manufacturer's order.
- Set the bread machine to the Italian Bread/Sandwich option & Medium crust.
- START the program.
- Let the cycle run completely.
- When the bread is done, take it out of the basket and leave it for five minutes to cool.
- Shake the bucket gently to dislodge the loaves.
- Let cool before slicing and serving.

1.7. Best-Ever Wheat Sandwich Bread

PREP.: 20 MINUTES | COOK: 3 HOURS

SERVING: 1 LB. - 4 SLICES | 1.5 LBS.- 6 SLICES | 2 LBS. - 8 SLICES.

PER SERVING: CALORIES 319 | TOTAL FAT 9G | PROTEIN 6G | CARBS 25G

Ingredient	1 Lb.	1.5 Lbs.	2 Lbs.
o Light Buttermilk	1 cup	1 1/3 cups	1 2/3 cups
o Dry Milk	2 teaspoons	1 tablespoon	1 tablespoon + 1 teaspoon
o Bread machine yeast	1 teaspoon	1 1/2 teaspoons	2 teaspoons
o Extra Virgin Olive Oil	1 tablespoon	2 tablespoons	2 2/3 tablespoons
o White Whole-Wheat Flour	1 tablespoon	1 3/4 tablespoons	2 1/3 tablespoons
o Dry milk	2 teaspoons	1 tablespoon	1 tablespoon + 1 teaspoon
o Local honey	2 tablespoons	3 tablespoons	4 tablespoons
o Light Buttermilk	1 cup	1 1/3 cups	1 2/3 cups
o Bread flour	1 ¼ cups	1 3/4 cups	2 ½ cups

Directions:

- Follow the directions provided, with an emphasis on referring to the bread machine's manual.
- Add all ingredients to the basket of the machine by following the manufacturer's order.
- If using the delay timer, make a small indentation in the flour for the yeast to ensure it doesn't come into contact with the liquid below.
- Start the bread machine as per the manufacturer's instructions, choosing the right settings for bread type, crust color, and loaf size.
- Monitor the bread machine throughout the process. Once baking is complete, the machine will signal the end.
- Carefully open the top, use the oven gloves or a cloth to take out the bread pan.
- Allow the bread to rest for 5-7 minutes before transferring it to a wire rack. Once cooled completely, slice and enjoy.
- Always refer to your bread machine's manual for the best results. Remember to refer to your bread machine's handbook and settings for correct instructions, as different models' processes and settings may vary.

1.8. Buttermilk Bread

PREP.: 20 MINUTES | COOK: 2 TO 4 HOURS

SERVING: 1 LB. - 6 SLICES | 1.5 LBS.- 9 SLICES | 2 LBS. – 12 SLICES.

PER SERVING: CALORIES 180 | TOTAL FAT 2G | PROTEIN 3G | CARBS 19G

Ingredient	1 Lb.	1.5 Lbs.	2 Lbs.
o Salt	1/2 teaspoon	3/4 teaspoon	1 teaspoon
o Active Dry Yeast	1 1/2 teaspoons	2 1/4 teaspoons	2 3/4 teaspoons
o White Sugar	1 tablespoon	1 1/2 tablespoons	2 tablespoons
o Buttermilk	¾ cup	1 1/8 cup	1 ½ cups
o Whole Wheat Flour	1 1/4 cups	1 3/4 cups	2 1/2 cups
o Margarine	2 teaspoons	1 tablespoon	1 ¼ tablespoons

Directions:

- Follow the order of the list and add all the ingredients inside the bread machine.
- Choose the "White Bread" cycle or equivalent on your bread machine.
- Allow the bread to complete its baking cycle.
- Once done, carefully remove the pan and let it cool for five minutes.
- Gently jiggle the bread pan to release the loaf.
- Place the bread onto a wire rack & let it cool before slicing.

PREP.: 20 MINUTES| COOK: 2 TO 3 HOURS

SERVING: 1 LB. - 6 SLICES|1.5 LBS.- 8 SLICES| 2 LBS. – 10 SLICES.

PER SERVING: CALORIES 224 | TOTAL FAT 4G | PROTEIN 6G | CARBS 41G

Ingredient	1 Lb.	1.5 Lbs.	2 Lbs.
o White Flour	1 1/2 cups	2 1/4 cups	3 cups
o Salt	1/2 teaspoon	3/4 teaspoon	1 teaspoon
o Water	2/3 cup	1 cup	1 1/3 cups
o Whole Egg, beaten	1/2	1	1 1/2
o Vegetable Oil	1 1/2 teaspoons	1 tablespoon	1 1/3 tablespoons
o Rye Flour	2 tablespoons	¼ cup	¼ cup
o Honey	1 1/8 teaspoons	1 1/2 tablespoons	2 tablespoons
o Dry Yeast	1/2 teaspoon	3/4 teaspoon	1 teaspoon

Directions:

- Add all ingredients to the basket of the machine by following the manufacturer's order.
- Set the machine to the "Basic/White Bread" setting with a medium crust.
- Press START and allow the bread to bake for the duration of the cycle.
- Once finished, remove the loaf and let it cool for 5 minutes.
- Gently jiggle the loaf out of the pan.

PREP.: 10 MINUTES | COOK: 30 TO 40 MINUTES

SERVING: 1 LB. - 4 SLICES|1.5 LBS.- 6 SLICES| 2 LBS. – 8 SLICES.

PER SERVING: CALORIES 236 | TOTAL FAT 20G | PROTEIN 6G | CARBS 16G

Ingredient	1 Lb.	1.5 Lbs.	2 Lbs.
o Baking Powder	1/2 teaspoon	3/4 teaspoon	1 teaspoon
o Softened Cream Cheese	1/3 cup	1/2 cup	2/3 cup
o Heavy Whipping Cream	5 tablespoons	6 1/2 tablespoons	8 tablespoons
o Melted Coconut Oil	3 tablespoons	1/4 cup	1/3 cup
o Almond Flour	1/4 cup	1/2 cup	2/3 cup
o Flaxseed	2 tablespoons	1/4 cup	1/4 cup
o Coconut Flour	5 tablespoons	6 1/2 tablespoons	8 tablespoons
o Sesame Seeds	1 1/3 tablespoons	2 2/3 tablespoons	3 1/2 tablespoons
o Salt	1/6 teaspoon	1/4 teaspoon	1/3 teaspoon
o Eggs	2	3	4
o Ground Psyllium Husk Powder	2 teaspoons	2 tablespoons	2 2/3 tablespoons
o Ground Caraway Seeds	1/6 teaspoon	1/2 teaspoon	2/3 teaspoon

Directions:

- In a bowl, whisk together the eggs, whipping cream, cream cheese, and coconut oil.
- In a different bowl, mix the flours and then add the remaining ingredients.
- Add the wet mixture to the bread machine first, followed by the dry mixture.
- Choose the "BASIC/WHITE" setting or a low-carb/grain-free setting if available. Allow the bread to bake for the designated time.
- Once baked, remove the bread, cool for 5 to 7 minutes.
- Gently jiggle the pan to release the loaf.
- Let the bread cool on a wire rack, slice, and serve.

2.1. Butter Bread Rolls

PREP.: 10 MINUTES | COOK: 50 MINUTES

SERVING: 1 LB. – 12 ROLLS|1.5 LBS.-18 ROLLS| 2 LBS. – 24 ROLLS

PER SERVING: CALORIES 138 | TOTAL FAT 2G | PROTEIN 4G | CARBS 38G

Ingredient	1 Lb.	1.5 Lbs.	2 Lbs.
o Warm Milk	3/4 cup	1 1/8 cups	1 1/2 cups
o Butter or Margarine, softened	3 tablespoons	1/4 cup + 1 tablespoon	1/3 cup + 1tablespoon
o Sugar	3 tablespoons	1/4 cup + 2tablespoons	1/3 cup + 1tablespoon
o Active Dry Yeast	1 teaspoon	1 1/2 teaspoons	2 teaspoons
o Salt	1/2 teaspoon	3/4 teaspoon	1 teaspoon
o Bread Flour	2 1/2 cups	3 3/4 cups	5 cups
o Eggs	1	1	1 1/2

Directions:

- Follow the manufacturer's recommended order and add all ingredients to the basket of the bread machine.
- Choose the dough setting.
- When the cycle ends, flip the dough onto a floured surface.
- Separate the dough as follows:
- - Per 1 lb.: Divide into 12 equal parts.
- - Per 1.5 lbs.: Divide into 18 equal parts.
- - Per 2 lbs.: Divide into 24 equal parts.
- Form the dough into balls.
- Place in a buttered 13-by-9-inch baking dish.
- Let it rise in a warm location for 30-45 minutes, covered.
- Let it bake for 13-16 minutes, or until golden brown, at 350°F.
- Serve and enjoy.

PREP TIME: 10 MINUTES | COOK TIME: 2 HOURS |

SERVES: 1 LB. 6 BAGELS|1,5 LBS.9 BAGELS|2 LBS. 12 BAGELS

PER SERVING: CALORIES 74 | TOTAL FAT 0.2G | PROTEIN 2.3G | CARBS 16G

Ingredient	**1 Lb.**	**1.5 Lbs.**	**1 Lbs.**
o *Salt*	3/4 teaspoon	1 teaspoon	1 1/2 teaspoons
o *Egg Wash Mixture*	See note	See note	See note
o *Sugar (Granulated)*	1/2 tablespoon	3/4 tablespoon	1 tablespoon
o *Water (Warm)*	1/2 cup + 2 tablespoons	3/4 cup + 1 tablespoon	1 cup + 1 1/2 tablespoons
o *All-Purpose Flour (Gluten-Free)*	1 3/4 cups	2 5/8 cups	3 1/2 cups
o *Active dry yeast*	1 teaspoon	1 1/2 teaspoons	2 teaspoons
o **Toppings*	At will	At will	At will

Note: *Egg wash mixture (1 egg and 1 tbsp. of water whisked together)

*Your preferred toppings like sesame seeds, shredded cheese, poppy seeds, coarse salt, and more

Directions:

- Place the water, flour, sugar finally salt in the basket of the bread machine. Follow the ingredient list in this sequence.
- Make an indentation in the middle of the dry ingredients with your finger.
- Fill the well with dry yeast, then top with flour.
- Close the lid of the bread machine, press "start" after selecting the "dough" setting.
- After the dough is made, punch it down in the pan and let it rest for 10 minutes.
- Remove the dough & divide as follows:
- For 1 lb.: Divide into 6 equal parts.
- For 1.5 lbs.: Divide into 9 equal parts.
- For 2 lbs.: Divide into 12 equal parts.
- Make each portion into a round shape. Using gluten-free flour on your hands, shape the balls into bagel rings.
- Put bagels on a floured surface and put a damp kitchen towel on top. Allow to rest for almost 10 minutes.
- Let the oven preheat to 425°F and place parchment paper on a baking sheet.
- Boil water in a saucepan.
- With a slotted spoon, add 2 to 3 bagels to the boiling water. Cook for 1-2 minutes, flip and cook another 1-2 minutes. (Longer boiling results in chewier bagels.)
- Place cooked bagels on a baking sheet, brush with egg wash, & add desired toppings.
- Let them bake for 20 minutes. Cool before serving.

2.3. Raisin Muffins

PREP TIME: 20 MINUTES | COOK TIME: 1 1/2 HOURS

SERVES: 1 LB. 6 MUFFINS | 1,5 LBS. 9 MUFFINS | 2 LBS. 12 MUFFINS.

PER SERVING: CALORIES 293 | TOTAL FAT 13G | PROTEIN 4G | CARBS 39G

Ingredient	1 Lb.	1.5 Lbs.	2 Lbs.
For dough:			
o Milk	1/4 cup	3/8 cup	1/2 cup
o Butter	3 tablespoons	1/4 cup	1/4 cup
o Eggs	1	1	1 ½
o Sugar	1 1/2 tablespoons	2 tablespoons	2 1/2 tablespoons
o All-Purpose Flour	1 1/4 cups	1 3/4 cups	2 1/2 cups
o Active Dry Yeast	1/2 teaspoon	3/4 teaspoon	1 teaspoon
o Salt	1/4 teaspoon	3/8 teaspoon	1/2 teaspoon
After beeping:			
o Raisins	1/2 cup	3/4 cup	1 cup
For filling:			
o Butter	1/4 cup	3/8 cup	1/2 cup
o Powdered Sugar	1 teaspoon	1 1/2 teaspoons	2 teaspoons
o Vanilla Sugar	1 teaspoon	1 1/2 teaspoons	2 teaspoons
o Vanilla Pudding	1/2 cup	3/4 cup	1 cup

Directions:

- Put the ingredients for the dough in the bread machine and choose the dough setting.
- Add raisins when the machine indicates or after the first kneading cycle.
- When the cycle is complete, allow the dough to rise and rest for 45 minutes.
- For the 1 lb. batch, divide the dough into 6 equal portions. For the 1.5 lbs. batch, divide into 9 portions. For the 2 lbs. batch, divide into 12 portions. Place the divided dough into buttered muffin cups. Let rest for an additional 30 minutes.
- Let the oven preheat to 400°F (200°C).
- Bake for 20 minutes. Remove and allow to cool.
- For the filling, whisk together the powdered sugar, butter, and vanilla sugar. Once fluffy, gradually incorporate the prepared vanilla pudding.
- Slice the cooled muffins in half and spread the vanilla filling on the bottom half. Replace the top half and serve.

2.4. Breakfast Fruit Buns

PREP.: 20 MINUTES | COOK: 60 MINUTES

SERVES: 1 LB. 6 BUNS|1,5 LBS. 9 BUNS|2 LBS. 12 BUNS.

PER SERVING: CALORIES 266 | TOTAL FAT 5G | PROTEIN 7G | CARBS 48G

Ingredient	1 Lb.	1.5 Lbs.	2 Lbs.
For dough:			
o Water	1 cup	1.5 cups	2 cups
o Egg	1	1	1 ½
o Butter	1/4 cup	1/4 cup	1/4 cup
o Sugar	1/3 cup	1/3 cup	1/3 cup
o All-Purpose Flour	3 1/4 cups	3 3/4 cups	4 1/4 cups
o Lemon Zest	1/2 teaspoon	1/2 teaspoon	1/2 teaspoon
o Active Dry Yeast	1 1/2 teaspoons	1 1/2 teaspoons	1 1/2 teaspoons
o Salt	1/2 teaspoon	1/2 teaspoon	1/2 teaspoon
After beeping:			
o Dried Apricots	2 tablespoons	2 tablespoons	2 tablespoons
o Raisins	2 tablespoons	2 tablespoons	2 tablespoons
o Candied Cherries	2 tablespoons	2 tablespoons	2 tablespoons
o Candied Fruits	2 tablespoons	2 tablespoons	2 tablespoons
o Warm Milk (for brushing)	2/3 cup	2/3 cup	2/3 cup
o Sugar (for brushing)	1/3 cup	1/3 cup	1/3 cup

Directions:

- Put the ingredients for the dough in the bread machine and choose the dough setting.
- Add the mixed dried fruits when the machine indicates or after the first kneading cycle.
- Once the cycle completes, transfer dough to a floured surface. For the 1 lb. batch, divide the dough into 6 equal portions. For the 1.5 lbs. batch, divide into 9 portions. For the 2-pound batch, divide into 12 portions. With each portion, form a bun.
- Shape each portion into a bun and place on an oil sprayed parchment-lined baking sheet. Place a damp cloth on top and let them rise for 30 minutes.
- Brush the risen buns with a mixture of warm milk and sugar (1/3 cup sugar & 2/3 cup milk).
- Preheat the oven to 400°F and bake buns until golden brown or for 18-22 minutes.
- Remove and serve.

PREP.: 10 MINUTES | COOK: 3 HOURS

SERVES: 1 LB. 4-6 SLICES | 1,5 LBS. 6-9 SLICES | 2 LBS. 8-12 SLICES

PER SERVING: CALORIES 210 | TOTAL FAT 3G | PROTEIN 5G | CARBS 45G

Ingredient	1 Lb.	1.5 Lbs.	2 Lbs.
o Orange Juice	3/4 cup	1 cup	1 1/4 cups
o Egg	1	1	1 ½
o Margarine	3/4 tablespoon	1 tablespoon	1 1/4 tablespoons
o Hot Water	approx. 3 tablespoons	1/4 cup	1/3 cup
o Bread Flour	2 3/4 cups	3 1/2 cups	4 1/4 cups
o White Sugar	approx. 3 tablespoons	1/4 cup	approx. 5 tablespoons
o Orange Zest	1 1/2 tablespoons	2 tablespoons	2 1/2 tablespoons
o Salt	3/4 teaspoon	1 teaspoon	1 1/4 teaspoons
o Active Dry Yeast	1 1/2 teaspoons	1 3/4 teaspoons	2 teaspoons

Directions:

- Follow the manufacturer's recommended order and put the ingredients for the dough in the bread machine a.
- Select the basic or white bread setting.
- Start the bread machine.
- When cooked, carefully remove the baking tray & let the bread to cool for 10 minutes.
- Serve!

PREP.: 20 MINUTES | COOK: 2 HOURS

SERVES: 1 LB. 4-6 ROLLS|1,5 LBS. 6-9 ROLLS|2 LBS. 8-12 ROLLS

PER SERVING: CALORIES 185 | TOTAL FAT 6G | PROTEIN 5G | CARBS 29G

Ingredient	1 Lb.	1.5 Lbs.	2 Lbs.
For dough:			
o Cornstarch	1/4 cup	1/3 cup	1/2 cup less 1 tablespoon
o Eggs	1	1 1/2 (1 egg + 1 yolk)	2
o Vanilla Extract	3/4 teaspoon	1 teaspoon	1 1/4 teaspoons
o Granulated Sugar	1/4 cup	1/3 cup	.1/2 cup less 1 tablespoon
o Salt	1/2 teaspoon	3/4 teaspoon	1 teaspoon
o Butter (cubed)	3 tablespoons	4 tablespoons	5 tablespoons
o Bread Flour	2 1/4 cups	3 cups	3 3/4 cups
o Milk	1/3 cup	½ cup	2/3 cup
o Active Dry Yeast	1 1/2 teaspoons	1 3/4 teaspoons	2 teaspoons
For filling:			
o Ground Cinnamon	1 1/2 teaspoons	2 teaspoons	2 1/2 teaspoons
o Brown Sugar	3 tablespoons	1/4 cup	1/3 cup less 1 tablespoon
o Granulated Sugar	2 1/4 tablespoons	3 tablespoons	3 3/4 tablespoons
For brushing:			
o Melted Butter	3/4 tablespoon	1 tablespoon	1 1/4 tablespoons

Directions:

- Put the ingredients for the dough in the bread machine and choose the dough setting.
- Select the "dough program" and start the machine.
- While the dough is being prepared, mix filling ingredients in a bowl.
- Once the cycle is complete, divide the dough as per the serving size (1 lb. batch into 6 parts, 1.5 lb. batch into 9 parts, and 2 lb. batch into 12 parts). Let them rest for 10 minutes wrapped in plastic.
- When the dough is rolled out, it is brushed with butter (melted) and dusted with the cinnamon-sugar mixture.
- Roll the dough tightly, sealing the edges.
- Cut into rolls according to the desired batch size.
- Place in a greased baking dish and let them rise for half an hour.
- Let the oven preheat to 350°F and bake the rolls for half an hour.
- Serve warm and enjoy.

PREP.: 15 MINUTES | COOK: 3 HOURS 45 MINUTES

SERVES: 1 LB. 6 SLICES|1,5 LBS. 8 SLICES|2 LBS. 12 SLICES

PER SERVING: CALORIES 172 | TOTAL FAT 4G | PROTEIN 3G | CARBS 30G

Ingredient		1 Lb.	1.5 Lbs.	2 Lbs.
o	Water	1 cup	1 1/4 cups	1 1/2 cups
o	Vanilla Extract	1 teaspoon	1 1/4 teaspoons	1 1/2 teaspoons
o	Bread Flour	2 1/2 cups	3 1/4 cups	4 cups
o	Salt	1 teaspoon	1 1/4 teaspoons	1 1/2 teaspoons
o	Cocoa Powder	3 tablespoons	4 tablespoons	1/4 cup
o	Instant Yeast	1 teaspoon	1 1/4 teaspoons	1 1/2 teaspoons
o	Chocolate Chips	2/3 cup	3/4 cup	1 cup

Directions:

- Except for the chocolate chips, put all ingredients in the bread maker pan.
- Select the Sweetbread cycle and start the machine.
- Add chocolate chips when 3 minutes are left in the second kneading cycle.
- When cooked, take the loaf out and cool on a wire rack.

2.8. Sweet Pineapple Bread

PREP.: 15 MINUTES | COOK: 2 HOURS 15 MINUTES

SERVES: 1 LB. 4 SLICES|1,5 LBS. 6 SLICES|2 LBS. 8 SLICES

PER SERVING: CALORIES 144 | TOTAL FAT 9G | PROTEIN 6G | CARBS 18G

Ingredient	1 Lb.	1.5 Lbs.	2 Lbs.
o *Dried Pineapples*	8 oz.	12 oz.	16 oz.
o *Raisins*	1/2 cup	3/4 cup	1 cup
o *Wheat Flour*	1 cup	1 1/2 cups	2 cups
o *Eggs*	3	3	3
o *Baking Powder*	3 tsps.	4 1/2 tsps.	6 tsps.
o *Brown Sugar*	1 cup	1 1/2 cups	2 cups
o *Sugar*	1/4 cup	3/8 cup	1/2 cup
o *Vanilla Essence*	As required	As required	As required

Directions:

- Soak the raisins in warm water for 20 minutes.
- Add sifted wheat flour, brown sugar, vanilla extract & baking powder to a bowl.
- Add the soaked raisins and pineapples.
- In another bowl, whisk the eggs with sugar until creamy.
- Combine the egg mixture with the flour mixture.
- Add the combined mix to the bread machine and select the Basic/White Bread program.
- Once baked, allow the bread to cool for 1 hour under a towel.

PREP.: 15 MINUTES | COOK: 3 HOURS

SERVES: 1 LB. 8 SLICES|1,5 LBS.12 SLICES|2 LBS.16 SLICES

PER SERVING: CALORIES 290 | TOTAL FAT 9G | PROTEIN 4G | CARBS 42G

Ingredient	1 Lb.	1.5 Lbs.	2 Lbs.
o Large Eggs (beaten)	3 large eggs	4 large eggs	6 large eggs
o Sugar	1 1/3 cups	2 cups	2 2/3 cups
o Melted Butter	1/2 cup	3/4 cup	1 cup
o All-Purpose Flour	2 cups	3 cups	4 cups
o Zest of lemons	Zest of 2 Lemons	Zest of 3 Lemons	Zest of 4 Lemons
o 2% Milk	1/3 cup	½ cup	2/3 cup
o Vanilla Extract	1 teaspoon	1 1/2 teaspoons	2 teaspoons
o Baking Powder	3 teaspoons	4 ½ teaspoons	6 teaspoons

For the Glaze:

	1 Lb.	1.5 Lbs.	2 Lbs.
o Powdered Sugar	1 cup	1 1/2 cups	2 cups
o Fresh Lemon Juice	2 tablespoons	3 tablespoons	4 tablespoons

Directions:

- Mix powdered sugar and lemon juice for the glaze and set aside.
- Add all cake ingredients in the order specified to the bread machine pan.
- Select the Sweetbread cycle with a medium crust and start the machine.
- Once baked, let the cake cool on a rack.
- Drizzle with the prepared glaze before serving.

2.10. Cranberry Walnut Bread

PREP.: 15 MINUTES | COOK: 2 HOURS

SERVES: 1 LB. 4 SLICES | 1,5 LBS. 6 SLICES | 2 LBS. 8 SLICES

PER SERVING: CALORIES 184 | TOTAL FAT 5G | PROTEIN 5G | CARBS 31G

Ingredient	1 Lb.	1.5 Lbs.	2 Lbs.
o Water	1/4 cup	3/8 cup	1/2 cup
o Rolled Oats	1/4 cup	3/8 cup	1/2 cup
o Egg	1 egg	1 egg	1 egg
o Buttermilk	1 cup	1 1/2 cups	2 cups
o Margarine	1-1/2 tablespoons	2 1/4 tablespoons	3 tablespoons
o Honey	3 tablespoons	4 1/2 tablespoons	6 tablespoons
o Sugar	¼ cup	3/8 cup	½ cup
o Bread Flour	3 cups	4 1/2 cups	6 cups
o Salt	1 teaspoon	1 1/2 teaspoons	2 teaspoons
o Ground Cinnamon	1/2 teaspoon	3/4 teaspoon	1 teaspoon
o Chopped Walnuts	½ cup	¾ cup	1 cup
o Dried Cranberries	3/4 cup	1 1/8 cups	1 1/2 cups
o Active Dry Yeast	2 teaspoons	3 teaspoons	1 tablespoon
o Baking Soda	1/4 teaspoon	3/8 teaspoon	1/2 teaspoon

Directions:

- Add all ingredients except walnuts and cranberries to the bread machine pan.
- Select the sweet cycle with a light crust and start the machine.
- Add walnuts and cranberries when the machine beeps.
- Once baked, take the bread out from the pan and let it cool for ten minutes before serving.

3.1. 100% Whole Wheat Bread

PREP.: 35 MINUTES | COOK: 2 HOURS

SERVES: 1 LB. 4 SLICES | 1,5 LBS. 6 SLICES | 2 LBS. 8 SLICES

PER SERVING: CALORIES 147 | TOTAL FAT 6G | PROTEIN 4G | CARBS 22G

Ingredients	1 Lb.	1.5 Lbs.	2 Lbs.
o Lukewarm Water	3/4 cup	1 cup	1 1/4 cups
o Vegetable Oil or Olive Oil	1 tablespoon	1 1/2 tablespoons	2 tablespoons
o Honey or Maple Syrup	2 tablespoons	3 tablespoons	1/4 cup
o Table Salt	1 teaspoon	1 1/4 teaspoons	1 1/2 teaspoons
o Whole Wheat Flour	2 cups	3 cups	3 1/2 cups
o Sesame, Sunflower, or Flax Seeds (optional)	2 tablespoons	3 tablespoons	1/4 cup
o Bread Machine Yeast	3/4 teaspoon	1 teaspoon	1 1/2 teaspoons

Directions:

- Determine the size of the loaf you want to create and measure your ingredients.
- In the sequence listed above, add the ingredients to the bread pan.
- Cover the pan after placing it inside the bread maker.
- Start the bread machine. Choose the Whole Wheat/Wholegrain option, followed by the loaf size and, finally, the crust color. Begin the procedure.
- Remove the pan from the machine once the operation is complete and the bread is baked.
- Remove the bread from the pan and cool for at least 10 minutes on a wire rack before slicing.

PREP.: 15 MINUTES | COOK: 1 HOUR 30 MINUTES

SERVES: 1 LB. 4 SLICES|1,5 LBS. 6 SLICES|2 LBS.8 SLICES

PER SERVING: CALORIES 223 | TOTAL FAT 4G | PROTEIN 9G | CARBS 40G

Ingredients	1 Lb.	1.5 Lbs.	2 Lbs.
o *Milk*	3/4 cup	1 1/8 cups	1 1/4 cups
o *Sugar*	1 tablespoon	1 1/2 tablespoons	2 tablespoons
o *Olive Oil*	1 tablespoon	1 1/2 tablespoons	2 tablespoons
o *Salt*	1/2 teaspoon	3/4 teaspoon	1 teaspoon
o *Spelt Flour*	2 cups	3 cups	4 cups
o *Yeast*	1 1/4 teaspoons	1 7/8 teaspoons	2 1/2 teaspoons

Directions:

- In the bread machine, combine all of the ingredients according to the manufacturer's instructions.
- Start by selecting the basic bread setting, then light/medium crust. Remove the loaf pan from the machine after the loaf is finished baking.
- Allow for a 10-minute cooling period.
- Cut into slices and serve.

3.3. Honeyed Bulgur Bread

PREP.: 15 MINUTES | COOK: 2 HOURS 30 MINUTES

SERVES: 1 LB. 4 SLICES | 1,5 LBS. 6 SLICES | 2 LBS. 8 SLICES

PER SERVING: CALORIES 132 | TOTAL FAT 2G | PROTEIN 3G | CARBS 25G

Ingredient	1 Lb.	1.5 Lbs.	2 Lbs.
o Honey	2 tablespoons	3 tablespoons	1/4 cup
o Bulgur Wheat (extra coarse)	1/4 cup	1/3 cup	1/2 cup
o Boiling Water	1/4 cup	1/3 cup	1/2 cup
o Active Dry Yeast	2 teaspoons	2 1/4 teaspoons	1 tablespoon
o Salt	1 teaspoon	1 1/2 teaspoon	2 teaspoons
o Bread Flour	1/2 cup	3/4 cup	1 cup
o Vegetable Oil	1 tablespoon	1 1/2 tablespoon	2 tablespoons
o All-Purpose Flour	1 1/4 cups	1 1/2 cups	2 cups
o Water	3/4 cup	3/4 cup	1 cup
o Skim Milk	1 tablespoon	1/2 tablespoon	1/2 tablespoon

Directions:

- Place all essential ingredients in the bread machine's container in the manufacturer's recommended order.
- On your bread maker, select the basic cycle. This cycle is widely employed in traditional bread recipes. Check the handbook for any special suggestions for the basic cycle. After selecting the cycle, hit the start button to start the bread-making process.
- Depending on the cycle, the bread machine will handle the dough's mixing, kneading, rising, and baking. Depending on your machine and the selected cycle, the process will take a few hours. During the cycle, you may hear alarms or indications indicating when to add mix-ins or when the bread is done.
- When the bread machine finishes the cycle, it may indicate the bread is ready. Open the lid carefully and remove the bread pan out of the machine using oven mitts or a cloth. Take care since the pan and the bread inside will be hot.
- Let the bread cool for a few minutes in the pan. Then, gently shake or tap the pan with oven mitts to release the bread. Place the bread on a cooling rack to cool entirely. This will help keep the crust from turning mushy as a result of trapped steam.
- After the bread has cooled, slice it and serve it.
- Remember that bread machines vary in terms of settings and choices, so always refer to the handbook for your specific machine for the most up-to-date instructions.

3.4. Quinoa Whole Wheat Bread

PREP.: 10 MINUTES | COOK: 3 HOURS

SERVES: 1 LB. 8 SLICES|1,5 LBS. 12 SLICES|2 LBS.16 SLICES

PER SERVING: CALORIES 136 | TOTAL FAT 2G | PROTEIN 5G | CARBS 27G

Ingredient	1 Lb.	1.5 Lbs.	2 Lbs.
o Honey	1.1/2 tablespoons	2 tablespoons	2.1/2 tablespoons
o Water	1 cup	1.1/2 cups	2 cups
o Olive Oil	3/4 tablespoon	1.13 tablespoons	1.5 tablespoons
o Salt	1/4 teaspoon	3/8 teaspoon	1/2 teaspoon
o Whole Wheat Flour	7/8 cup	1 and 5/16 cups	1 and 3/4 cups
o Bread Flour	7/8 cup	1 and 5/16 cups	1 and 3/4 cups
o Toasted Sesame Oil	Pinch	Pinch	Pinch
o Uncooked Quinoa	1/6 cup	1/4 cup	1/3 cup
o Active Dry Yeast	3/4 teaspoon	1 and 1/8 teaspoons	1 and 1/2 teaspoons

Directions:

- Place all essential ingredients in the bread machine's container in the manufacturer's recommended order.
- Choose a basic, light crust and press the start button.
- When the bread machine finishes the cycle, it may indicate the bread is ready. Open the lid carefully and remove the bread pan out of the machine using oven mitts or a cloth. Take care since the pan and the bread inside will be hot.
- Let the bread cool for a few minutes in the pan. Then, gently shake or tap the pan with oven mitts to release the bread. Place the bread on a cooling rack to cool entirely.
- After the bread has cooled, slice it and serve it.

3.5. Buckwheat Bread

PREPARATION TIME: 10 MINUTES | COOKING TIME: 2 HOURS 40 MINUTES

SERVES: 1 LB. 8 SLICES | 1,5 LBS. 12 SLICES | 2 LBS. 16 SLICES

PER SERVING: CALORIES 660 | TOTAL FAT 21G | PROTEIN 14G | CARBS 48G

Ingredient	1 Lb.	1.5 Lbs.	2 Lbs.
o Sea Salt	1/4 teaspoon	1/3 teaspoon	1/2 teaspoon
o Soy Lecithin	1/4 teaspoon	1/3 teaspoon	1/2 teaspoon
o Active Dry Yeast	3/4 teaspoon	1 and 1/4 teaspoon	1 and 1/2 teaspoon
o Xanthan Gum	3/4 teaspoon	1 and 1/4 teaspoon	1 and 1/2 teaspoon
o Butter (softened)	2 teaspoons	1 tablespoon and 1/2 teaspoon	2 tablespoons
o Buckwheat Flour	1/8 cup	3/16 cup	1/4 cup
o Potato Starch	1/8 cup	3/16 cup	1/4 cup
o Tapioca Flour	1/8 cup	3/16 cup	1/4 cup
o Brown Rice Flour	1/4 cup	1/2 cup	3/4 cup
o Milk (at 110°F)	1/4 cup	1/2 cup	3/4 cup
o Eggs	1	1	2

Directions:

- Check the manufacturer's directions for your bread machine and fill the bread pan appropriately. Normally, you would add the wet ingredients first, followed by the dry ones.
- If your bread maker has a "gluten-free" setting, use that. If not, bake white bread using the "basic" setting.
- When the bread machine finishes the cycle, it may indicate the bread is ready. Open the lid carefully and remove the bread pan out of the machine using oven mitts or a cloth. Take care since the pan and the bread inside will be hot. Put it aside for 10 minutes before slicing.
- After the bread has cooled, slice it and serve it.

3.6. Hearty Oatmeal Loaf

PREPARATION TIME: 10 MINUTES | COOKING TIME: 2 TO 3 HOURS |

SERVES: 1 LB. LOAF 4|1,5 LBS. LOAF 6|2 LBS. LOAF 8

PER SERVING: CALORIES 149 | TOTAL FAT 1G | PROTEIN 4G | CARBS 26G

Ingredient	1 Lb.	1.5 Lbs.	2 Lbs.
o *Water (80°F)*	1/2 cup	3/4 cup	1 cup
o *Melted Butter*	1 tablespoon	1.1/2 tablespoons	2 tablespoons
o *Sugar*	1 tablespoon	1.1/2tablespoons	2 tablespoons
o *Salt*	1/2 teaspoon	3/4 teaspoon	1 teaspoon
o *Quick Oats*	1/3 cup	1/2 cup	3/4 cup
o *White Bread Flour*	3/4 cup	1 and 1/8 cups	1 and 1/2 cups
o *Instant Yeast*	1/2 teaspoon	3/4 teaspoon	1 teaspoon

Directions:

- Add all ingredients to your bread machine, following the manufacturer's instructions.
- Set the bread machine to the Basic/White Bread setting and Medium crust.
- Start the program.
- Once the cycle completes, remove the loaf from the pan and let it cool for 5 minutes.
- Gently shake the pan to release the loaf.
- Place on a cooling rack. Slice and serve once cooled.
- Transfer to a cooling rack to cool before slicing and serving.

3.7. Awesome Multigrain Bread

PREP.: 20 MINUTES | COOK: 2 TO 3 HOURS

SERVES: 1 LB. LOAF 4|1,5 LBS. LOAF 6|2 LBS. LOAF 8

PER SERVING: CALORIES 175 | TOTAL FAT 2G | PROTEIN 4G | CARBS 27G

Ingredients	**1 Lb.**	**1.5 Lbs.**	**2 Lbs.**
o *Water (80°F)*	1/2 cup	3/4 cup	1 cup
o *Melted Butter*	1 teaspoon	1.5 teaspoons	2 teaspoons
o *Honey*	1/2 teaspoon	3/4 teaspoon	1 teaspoon
o *Salt*	1/4 teaspoon	3/8 teaspoon	1/2 teaspoon
o *Multigrain Flour*	1/3 cup	1/2 cup	3/4 cup
o *White Bread Flour*	2/3 cup	1 cup	1 and 1/3 cups
o *Active Dry Yeast*	1/2 teaspoon	3/4 teaspoon	1 teaspoon

Directions:

- Add all ingredients to your bread machine, following the manufacturer's instructions.
- Set the bread machine to the Basic/White Bread setting and Medium crust.
- Start the program.
- Once the cycle completes, remove the loaf from the pan and let it cool for 5 minutes.
- Gently shake the pan to release the loaf.
- Place on a cooling rack. Slice and serve once cooled.

PREP.: 20 MINUTES | COOK: 4 HOURS

SERVES: 1 LB. 8 SLICES|1,5 LBS. 12 SLICES|2 LBS.16 SLICES

PER SERVING: CALORIES 193 | TOTAL FAT 2G | PROTEIN 3G | CARBS 17G

Ingredients	1 Lb.	1.5 Lbs.	2 Lbs.
o Lukewarm Water (100°F)	2/3 cup	1 cup	1 and 1/3 cups
o Salt	1/2 teaspoon	3/4 teaspoon	1 teaspoon
o Dry Milk Powder	1 tablespoon	1 and 1/2 tablespoons	2 tablespoons
o Brown Sugar	1 tablespoon	1 and 1/2 tablespoons	2 tablespoons
o Molasses	1 tablespoon	1 and 1/2 tablespoons	2 tablespoons
o Butter	1 tablespoon	1 and 1/2 tablespoons	2 tablespoons
o Whole Wheat Flour	1/3 cup	1/2 cup	3/4 cup
o Bread Flour	7/8 cup	1 and 1/4 cups	1 and 3/4 cups
o Caraway Seeds	3/4 tablespoon	1 and 1/8 tablespoons	1 and 1/2 tablespoons
o Rye Flour	1/3 cup	1/2 cup	3/4 cup
o Active Dry Yeast	3/4 teaspoon	1 and 1/8 teaspoons	1 and 1/2 teaspoons

Directions:

- Fill the bread machine pan with lukewarm water, milk powder, brown sugar, salt, butter, whole wheat flour, rye flour, bread flour, molasses, caraway seeds, and yeast in the sequence recommended by the manufacturer.
- On your bread machine, choose the Grain setting. This setting is intended for bread recipes that include a combination of grains such as whole wheat and rye. Check your bread machine's handbook for any special Grain setting recommendations.
- In addition, on your bread machine, select the 2 lbs. loaf size. This ensures that the machine prepares the dough for the required size of the bread.
- After selecting the Grain option and the 2-pound loaf size, hit the start button to begin the bread-making process.
- When the cycle is finished, the bread machine may indicate that the bread is ready. Open the lid carefully and remove the bread pan out of the machine using oven mitts or a cloth. Be careful since the pan and the bread inside will be hot.
- Let the bread cool for a few minutes in the pan. Then, gently shake or tap the pan with oven mitts to release the bread. Place the bread on a cooling rack to cool entirely.
- After the bread has cooled, slice it and serve it.

3.9. Oat Bread

PREP.: 20 MINUTES | COOK: 2 HOURS

SERVES: 1 LB. 4 SLICES|1,5 LBS. 6 SLICES|2 LBS.8 SLICES

PER SERVING: CALORIES 110 | TOTAL FAT 2G | PROTEIN 4G | CARBS 19G

Ingredient	1 Lb.	1.5 Lbs.	2 Lbs.
o *Oats*	1/3 cup	1/2 cup	2/3 cup
o *Water*	1/2 cup	3/4 cup	1 1/2 cups
o *Butter or Margarine*	1 tablespoon	1 1/2 tablespoons	2 tablespoons
o *Honey*	1 tablespoon	1 1/2 tablespoons	1/4 cup
o *Salt*	1/2 teaspoon	3/4 teaspoon	1 teaspoon
o *Bread Flour*	1 5/8 cups	2 3/8 cups	3 1/4 cups
o *Active Dry Yeast*	1 ½ teaspoons	2 teaspoons	2 1/2 teaspoons

Directions:

- In the bread pan, combine all of the ingredients, using the least amount of liquid specified in the recipe.
- Select the basic and medium crust setting and press the start button.
- Take note of the dough. If the dough appears dry and inflexible after 5-10 minutes, or if your machine sounds like it's trying to knead it, add extra moisture 15 ml at a time until it forms a smooth, easy, elastic ball that is slightly tacky to the touch.
- After baking, take bread from the pan and place it on a cake rack to cool for some time before slicing.

PREP.: 20 MINUTES | COOK: 3 HOURS

SERVES: 1 LB. 4 SLICES|1,5 LBS. 6 SLICES|2 LBS.8 SLICES

PER SERVING: CALORIES 163 | TOTAL FAT 6G | PROTEIN 5G | CARBS 21G

Ingredients	1 Lb.	1.5 Lbs.	2 Lbs.
○ Warm Water (110°F)	1/2 cup	3/4 cup	1 cup
○ Dijon-style Mustard	1/4 cup	1/3 cup	1/2 cup
○ Olive Oil	1 tablespoon	1 1/2 tablespoons	2 tablespoons
○ Molasses	1 tablespoon	1 tablespoon	1 1/2 tablespoons
○ Unbleached All-Purpose Flour	2 1/4 cups	3 1/3 cups	4 1/2 cups
○ Rye Flour	3/4 cup	1 cup	1 1/4 cups
○ Whole Wheat Flour	3/4 cup	1 cup	1 1/4 cups
○ Vital Wheat Gluten	2 teaspoons	1 tablespoon	1 tablespoon
○ Active Dry Yeast	1 1/2 teaspoons	2 1/4 teaspoons	3 teaspoons

Directions:

- Assemble all the ingredients in the bread machine pan according to the manufacturer's directions.
- Select the basic or white bread setting and push the start button.
- After baking, take bread from the pan and place it on a cooling rack to cool for some time before slicing.

CHAPTER 4: HOLIDAY BREAD RECIPES

4.1. Challah

PREP TIME: 10 MINUTES | COOK TIME: 2 HOURS 20 MINUTES

SERVES: 1 LB. 4 SLICES|1,5 LBS. 6 SLICES|2 LBS.8 SLICES

PER SERVING: CALORIES 180 | TOTAL FAT 6G | PROTEIN 4G | CARBS 27G

Ingredient	1 Lb.	1.5 Lbs.	2 Lbs.
o All-Purpose/Bread Flour	2 and ¾ cups	3 and 1/2 cups	4 and 1/4 cups
o Water	1 cup	1 and 1/4 cups	1 and 1/2 cups
o Salt	3/4 teaspoon	1 teaspoon	1 and 1/8 teaspoons
o Brown Sugar	1/4 cup	1/3 cup	1/2 cup
o Active Dry Yeast	2 and 1/4 teaspoons	2 and 7/8 teaspoons	1 tablespoon
o Sesame or Poppy Seeds	As desired	As desired	As desired
o Whole Egg, lightly whisked	1/4 cup	1/3 cup	1/2 cup
o Egg Yolks	3	4	5
o Oil	1/4 cup	1/3 cup	1/3 cup

Notes: Challah is a rich braided, traditional Jewish loaf often eaten during Shabbat and holidays. Store in a bread bag or wrapped in a clean tea towel to maintain freshness. It can also be frozen for long-term storage.

Directions:

- Add all ingredients to the bread machine pan in the manufacturer's recommended order.
- Select the dough cycle and press start.
- Preheat oven to 350°F. Once the dough cycle completes, remove the dough from the machine.
- Divide dough in half, then further divide every half into three equal parts.
- Braid the three sections, and pinch both ends.
- Place on a greased baking sheet and cover. Let rise for 30 minutes.
- Brush with egg wash and add seeds on top (if desired).
- Bake for 30 minutes, or until golden brown. Serve and enjoy.

4.2. Greek Easter Bread

PREP: 10 MINUTES | COOK: 2 HOURS 30 MINUTES

SERVES: 1 LB. 4 SLICES | 1,5 LBS. 6 SLICES | 2 LBS. 8 SLICES

PER SERVING: CALORIES 220 | TOTAL FAT 9G | PROTEIN 5G | CARBS 30G

Ingredient	1 Lb.	1.5 Lbs.	2 Lbs.
o Caster Sugar	1/4 cup	1/3 cup	1/2 cup
o Whole Eggs, lightly whisked	2	3	4
o Dried Yeast	1 and 1/4 teaspoons	2 teaspoons	2 and 1/2 teaspoons
o Bread Flour	2 and 3/4 cups	3 and 1/4 cups	4 and 1/2 cups
o Salt	1/2 teaspoon	3/4 teaspoon	1 teaspoon
o Butter, melted	1/4 cup	1/3 cup	1/2 cup
o Milk	1/6 cup	1/4 cup	1/3 cup
o Lukewarm Water	1/6 cup	1/4 cup	1/3 cup
o Juice from half an Orange, Grated Rinds	As desired	As desired	As desired

Notes: For a richer flavor, consider adding flavorings such as vanilla or aniseed. You can also decorate the bread with sliced almonds or granulated sugar before baking for a traditional touch.

Directions:

- Add 1 tablespoon of caster sugar, the specific amount of lukewarm water for your chosen size, and the dried yeast into the bread machine pan. Mix lightly and let it rest for 8 minutes.
- Add the remaining ingredients to the pan.
- Choose the dough cycle and press start.
- Preheat the oven to 338°F. Grease a baking tray and line with parchment paper.
- After the dough cycle completes, remove the dough and divide it into three sections. Roll each section into long ropes and pinch one end together.
- Braid the ropes together and join ends to form a circle.
- Place dyed eggs (if using) in the braided dough and let rise for another 20 minutes.
- Brush with egg wash.
- Bake for 20 minutes or until golden brown.
- Serve and enjoy.

4.3. Christmas Bread

PREP: 10 MINUTES | COOK: 3 HOURS

SERVES: 1 LB. 4 SLICES|1,5 LBS. 6 SLICES|2 LBS.8 SLICES

PER SERVING: CALORIES 178 | TOTAL FAT 2G | PROTEIN 4G | CARBS 37G

Ingredient	1 Lb.	1.5 Lbs.	2 Lbs.
o *Warm Whole Milk (70°F to 80°F)*	1 cup	1 1/2 cups	2 cups
o *Lemon Juice*	1/4 teaspoon	1/3 teaspoon	1/2 teaspoon
o *Butter, softened*	1 tablespoon	1 ½ tablespoons	2 tablespoons
o *Sugar*	1 tablespoon	1 1/2 tablespoons	2 tablespoons
o *Salt*	3/4 teaspoon	1 1/8 teaspoons	1 ½ teaspoons
o *Bread Flour*	1 and 1/2 cups	2 and 1/4 cups	3 cups
o *Active Dry Yeast*	1 teaspoon	1 ½ teaspoons	2 teaspoons
o *Golden Raisins*	1/4 cup	3/8 cup	1/2 cup
o *Raisins*	1/4 cup	3/8 cup	1/2 cup
o *Dried Currants*	1/6 cup	1/4 cup	1/3 cup
o *Grated Lemon Zest*	1/2 teaspoon	3/4 teaspoon	1 teaspoon

For Glaze:

	1 Lb.	1.5 Lbs.	2 Lbs.
o *Powdered Sugar*	2 tablespoons	3 tablespoons	1/4 cup
o *2% Milk*	1 teaspoon	1 ½ teaspoons	2 teaspoons
o *Melted Butter*	1/2 teaspoon	1 teaspoon	1 ½ teaspoon
o *Vanilla Extract*	1/8 teaspoon	1/4 teaspoon	1/2 teaspoon

Directions:

- In the bread machine pan, combine the specified amount of sugar, the specified amount of warm milk for the chosen size, and the yeast. Mix lightly and let rest for 8 minutes.
- Add the remaining ingredients to the pan.
- Choose the dough cycle and press start.
- Preheat the oven to 335°F. Grease a baking tray and line with parchment paper.
- After the dough cycle completes, remove the dough and divide it into three sections. Roll each section into long ropes and pinch one end together.
- Braid the ropes together and join ends to form a circle.
- Place dyed eggs (if using) in the braided dough and let rise for another 20 minutes.
- Brush with egg wash.
- Bake for 20 minutes or until golden brown.
- Serve and enjoy.

PREP: 10 MINUTES | COOK: 3 HOURS

SERVES: 1 LB. 4 SLICES|1,5 LBS. 6 SLICES|2 LBS.8 SLICES

PER SERVING: CALORIES 202 | TOTAL FAT 4G | PROTEIN 5G | CARBS 36G

Ingredient	1 Lb.	1.5 Lbs.	2 Lbs.
o *Milk*	1/2 cup	3/4 cup	1 cup
o *Molasses*	2 tablespoons	3 tablespoons	1/4 cup
o *Egg*	1/2	3/4	1
o *Butter*	2 tablespoons	3 tablespoons	1/4 cup
o *Bread Flour*	1 and 1/3 cups	2 cups	2 and 2/3 cups
o *Brown Sugar*	2 teaspoons	1 tablespoon	1 and 1/2 tablespoons
o *Salt*	1/2 teaspoon	3/4 teaspoon	1 teaspoon
o *Ground Cinnamon*	1/2 teaspoon	3/4 teaspoon	1 teaspoon
o *Ground Ginger*	1/2 teaspoon	3/4 teaspoon	1 teaspoon
o *Active Dry Yeast*	1 and 1/8 teaspoons	1 and 1/2 teaspoons	2 teaspoons
o *Raisins*	1/6 cup	1/4 cup	1/3 cup

Directions:

- In the bread machine pan, combine the specified amount of brown sugar, the chosen amount of milk for your desired size, and the yeast. Mix lightly and let rest for 8 minutes.
- Add the molasses, egg, butter, bread flour, salt, ground cinnamon, ground ginger, and raisins to the pan in the order recommended by your bread machine manufacturer.
- Select the dough cycle and press start.
- If you are planning to bake in an oven (instead of a bread machine's baking cycle): Preheat the oven to 338°F. Grease a baking tray and line with parchment paper. Once the dough cycle completes, shape the dough as desired (e.g., into a loaf or braided form). Let it rise in a warm place for another 20 minutes. Brush with egg wash (if using). Bake for 20 minutes or until golden brown.
- Serve and enjoy.

PREP: 10 MINUTES | COOK: 4 HOURS

SERVES: 1 LB. 4 SLICES | 1,5 LBS. 6 SLICES | 2 LBS. 8 SLICES

PER SERVING: CALORIES 199 | TOTAL FAT 6G | PROTEIN 5G | CARBS 31G

Ingredient	**1 Lb.**	**1.5 Lbs.**	**2 Lbs.**
o *Water*	1/2 cup	3/4 cup	1 cup
o *Canned Pumpkin*	1/4 cup	3/8 cup	1/2 cup
o *Brown Sugar*	2 tablespoons	3 tablespoons	1/4 cup
o *Vegetable Oil*	1and 1/4 tablespoons	1 and 1/2 tablespoons	2 tablespoons
o *All-Purpose Flour*	1 and 1/3 cups	2 cups	2 and 1/2 cups
o *Whole-Wheat Flour*	2/3 cup	1 cup	1 and 1/3 cups
o *Salt*	1/2 teaspoon	3/4 teaspoon	1 teaspoon
o *Sweetened Dried Cranberries*	1/8 cup	1/4 cup	1/4 cup
o *Walnuts (chopped)*	1/8 cup	1/4 cup	1/4 cup
o *Active Dry Yeast*	1 and 1/2 teaspoons	1 and 3/4 teaspoons	2 and 1/4 teaspoons

Directions:

- Add all ingredients, except for the dried cranberries and walnuts, to the bread machine in the order specified by the manufacturer.
- Choose the sweet bread cycle with a light crust setting and start.
- Add sweetened dried cranberries and chopped walnuts just before the final kneading cycle.
- Once baking completes, remove the bread from the machine and let it cool on a rack.
- Serve and enjoy.

4.6. Portuguese Sweet Bread

PREP: 10 MINUTES | COOK: 3.5 HOURS

SERVES: 1 LB. 4 SLICES|1,5 LBS. 6 SLICES|2 LBS.8 SLICES

PER SERVING: CALORIES 180 | TOTAL FAT 6G | PROTEIN 5G | CARBS 30G

Ingredient	1 Lb.	1.5 Lbs.	2 Lbs.
o Evaporated Milk	1/2 cup	2/3 cup	3/4 cup
o Water	1/8 cup + 1 tablespoon	1/4 cup + 1 tablespoon	1/3 cup + 1 tablespoon
o Large Eggs	1	1.5	2
o Butter (Melted)	1 ¾ tablespoons	2 ¼ tablespoons	2 ¾ tablespoons
o Lemon Extract	1/3 teaspoon	1/2 teaspoon	3/4 teaspoon
o Vanilla Extract or Vanilla Powder	3/4 teaspoon	1 and 1/4 teaspoons	1 and 1/2 teaspoons
o Bread Flour	1 and 1/2 cups	2 and 1/4 cups	3 cups
o Light Brown Sugar	2 tablespoons	3 tablespoons	1/4 cup
o Instant Potato Flakes	1/2 teaspoon	3/4 teaspoon	1 teaspoon
o Gluten	1/4 teaspoon	3/8 teaspoon	1/2 teaspoon
o Salt	1/3 teaspoon	1/2 teaspoon	3/4 teaspoon
o Bread Machine Yeast	1/3teaspoon	1/2teaspoon	3/4 teaspoon

Directions:

- Place all the ingredients in the bread machine pan in the sequence specified by the manufacturer. Make sure you add them in the correct order. Set the crust option to "dark" and run the machine through the Basic or Sweet Bread cycle. To begin the baking process, press the Start button. Please keep in mind that this recipe cannot be used with the Delay Timer feature.
- When the baking cycle is finished, remove the bread from the machine's pan and place it on a cooling rack. Allow the bread to cool completely before slicing and serving.
- Portuguese Sweet Bread is a delectable dessert ideal for celebrating holidays or enjoying any time of year. Its creamy, buttery flavor with lemon and vanilla undertones makes it a flexible breakfast and dessert choice. For a morning treat, toast it with jam or lemon curd, or mix it with sweet wines for a fulfilling dessert experience.
- Please refer to your bread machine's handbook for detailed time information based on the Basic or Sweet Bread cycle. The baking time can normally range from 2.5 to 3.5 hours, depending on the parameters of your machine.

4.7. St. Patrick's Rum Bread

PREP: 30 MINUTES | COOK: 3 HOURS

LOAF: 1 LB. 4 |1,5 LBS. 6 |2 LBS.8

PER SERVING: CALORIES 170 | TOTAL FAT 4G | PROTEIN 4G | CARBS 31G

Ingredient	1 Lb.	1.5 Lbs.	2 Lbs.
o Whole Egg	1	1	1
o Rum Extract	1 tablespoon	1 tablespoon	1 tablespoon
o Bread Flour	2 cups	3 cups	4 cups
o Packed Brown Sugar	3 tablespoons	4.5 tablespoons	6 tablespoons
o Salt	1 and 1/4 teaspoons	1 and 7/8 teaspoons	2 and 1/2 teaspoons
o Ground Cinnamon	1/2 teaspoon	3/4 teaspoon	1 teaspoon
o Ground Nutmeg	1/4 teaspoon	3/8 teaspoon	1/2 teaspoon
o Ground Cardamom	1/4 teaspoon	3/8 teaspoon	1/2 teaspoon
o Bread Machine Yeast	1 teaspoon	1 and 1/2 teaspoons	2 teaspoons

For the topping:

Ingredient	1 Lb.	1.5 Lbs.	2 Lbs.
o Egg Yolk	1	1	1
o Pecans, chopped	1 and 1/2 teaspoons	1 and 1/2 teaspoons	1 and 1/2 teaspoons
o Brown Sugar	1 and 1/2 teaspoons	1 and 1/2 teaspoons	1 and 1/2 teaspoons

Directions:

- Crack an egg into a cup and add water until the mixture measures half a cup.
- Add the egg mixture to the machine.
- Follow the manufacturer's instructions when adding all of the ingredients to your bread maker.
- Set your bread machine's program to Basic/White Bread and the crust type to Medium.
- Press Start.
- Prepare the topping mixture and brush it over the bread when there are 40 minutes left in the cycle.
- Wait until the next cycle is finished.
- After baking, remove the bread bucket and let it cool for 5 minutes.
- To remove the loaf from the bucket, give it a light shake.
- Place on a cooling rack to cool before slicing and serving.

4.8. Raisin Cinnamon Swirl Bread

PREP: 10 MINUTES | COOK: 3 HOURS 20 MINUTES

LOAF: 1 LB. 4 |1,5 LBS. 6 |2 LBS.8

PER SERVING: CALORIES 297 | TOTAL FAT 10G | PROTEIN 5G | CARBS 46G

Ingredient	1 Lb.	1.5 Lbs.	2 Lbs.
For the Dough:			
o Milk	3 tablespoons	1/4 cup	1/4 cup
o *Large Egg, beaten	1/2	1	1
o Water	As required	As required	As required
o Butter, softened	3 tablespoons	1/4 cup	1/4 cup
o White Sugar	1/4 cup	1/3 cup	1/3 cup
o Salt	3/4 teaspoon	1 teaspoon	1 teaspoon
o Bread Flour	2 1/2 cups	3 1/2 cups	3 1/2 cups
o Active Dry Yeast	1 1/2 teaspoons	2 teaspoons	2 teaspoons
o Raisins	1/4 cup	1/2 cup	1/2 cup
For the Cinnamon Swirl:			
o White Sugar	1/4 cup	1/3 cup	1/3 cup
o Ground Cinnamon	2 teaspoons	3 teaspoons	3 teaspoons
o Egg Whites, beaten	1	2	2
o Butter, melted and cooled	1/4 cup	1/3 cup	1/3 cup

***Note:** When a recipe calls for a specific proportion of an egg (e.g., 2/3 or 1/2), you can simply beat the egg lightly and use the indicated amount of the beaten mixture. Careful measuring is recommended to ensure the best results.*

Directions:

- For the bread: In a small bowl, combine milk and egg.
- Add water to the mixture until you have 1 cup.
- Place the egg mixture in the bread machine's baking pan.
- Add the other ingredients (excluding raisins) in the manufacturer's recommended order.
- Close the bread machine lid after placing the baking pan inside.
- Select the Dough cycle.
- Press Start.
- Wait for the bread machine to beep before adding raisins. If your machine doesn't have this feature, add the raisins with other ingredients.
- After the Dough cycle completes, remove the dough and place on a lightly floured surface.
- Let it rest for 10 minutes.
- Roll the dough out to a rectangle.

- For the cinnamon swirl: In a small bowl, combine sugar and cinnamon. Consider adding additional raisins for a richer flavor and texture.
- Brush the rolled dough with beaten egg whites.
- Sprinkle the cinnamon-sugar mixture over the dough.
- Tightly roll the dough and seal the edges.
- Place the rolled dough into the baking pan and cover it.
- Let it rise in a warm place for 30 minutes.
- Bake in a preheated oven at 375°F for 25-30 minutes, or until golden brown.
- Remove from the oven and brush with melted butter.
- Cool on a wire rack before slicing.

4.9. Christmas Fruit Bread

PREP: 10 MINUTES | COOK: 3 HOURS 10 MINUTES

LOAF: 1 LB. 4 | 1,5 LBS. 6 | 2 LBS. 8

PER SERVING: CALORIES 310 | TOTAL FAT 9G | PROTEIN 4G | CARBS 41G

Ingredient	1 Lb.	1.5 Lbs.	2 Lbs.
o Sugar	1 tablespoon	1 1/2 tablespoons	2 1/4 tablespoons
o *Whole Egg	3/4	1	1 1/2
o Bread Machine Yeast	3/4 teaspoon	1 teaspoon	1 1/2 teaspoons
o Ground Cardamom	3/8 teaspoon	1/2 teaspoon	3/4 teaspoon
o Salt	3/4 teaspoon	1 teaspoon	1 1/2 teaspoons
o Water	1 cup	1 cup and 2 tablespoons	1 cup and 1 tablespoon
o Mixed Candied Fruit	1/4 cup	1/3 cup	2/3 cup
o Softened Butter	3 tablespoons	1/4 cup	1/4 cup
o Bread Flour	2 1/4 cups	3 cups	3 cups
o Raisins	1/4 cup	1/3 cup	2/3 cup

*Note: When a recipe calls for a specific proportion of an egg (e.g., 2/3 or 1/2), you can simply beat the egg lightly and use the indicated amount of the beaten mixture. Careful measuring is recommended to ensure the best results.

Directions:

- In the bread machine, combine all ingredients except the candied fruits and raisins in the order recommended by the manufacturer.
- Choose the basic cycle and medium crust. Start by pressing the start button.
- When your bread machine indicates it's time to add extras (usually a series of beeps), add the candied fruits and raisins.
- Once the baking cycle is complete, remove the bread from the machine and place it on a cooling rack. Let it cool for at least 30 minutes before slicing to allow the structure to set and to ensure clean slices.
- For a festive touch, you can sprinkle some powdered sugar on top or drizzle with a simple icing. Serve with butter or cream cheese for added richness.

4.10. Hungarian Spring Bread

PREP: 10 MINUTES | COOK: 4 HOURS

LOAF: 1 LB. 4 | 1.5 LBS. 6 | 2 LBS. 8

PER SERVING: CALORIES 389 | TOTAL FAT 13G | PROTEIN 9G | CARBS 47G

Ingredient	1 Lb.	1.5 Lbs.	2 Lbs.
For the dough:			
Sour cream, at room temperature	½ cup	¾ cup	1 cup
Buttermilk	¼ cup	⅓ cup	½ cup
Large egg	2/3 proportion*	1 large egg	1 large egg
Egg yolk	2/3 proportion*	1 yolk	2 yolks
Vanilla extract	1 teaspoon	1½ teaspoons	2 teaspoons
Almond extract	⅓ teaspoon	½ teaspoon	⅔ teaspoon
Softened unsalted butter or margarine	2 tablespoons	3 tablespoons	4 tablespoons
Bread flour	2 cups	3 cups	4 cups
Sugar	2⅔ tablespoons	¼ cup	⅓ cup
Salt	1 teaspoon	1½ teaspoons	2 teaspoons
Bread machine yeast	2 teaspoons	1 tablespoon	1 tablespoon + 1 teaspoon
Golden raisins	¼ cup	⅓ cup	½ cup
Diced lemon confit or candied lemon peel	¼ cup	⅓ cup	½ cup
Pecan pieces	2⅔ tablespoons	¼ cup	⅓ cup
Unbleached all-purpose flour	2 teaspoons	1 tablespoon	1 tablespoon + 1 teaspoon
For the lemon icing:			
Sifted confectioners' sugar	½ cup	¾ cup	1 cup
Grated lemon zest	⅔ teaspoon	1 teaspoon	1⅓ teaspoons
Fresh lemon juice	⅔ teaspoon	1 teaspoon	1⅓ teaspoons
Warm milk	⅔ to 1 tablespoon	1 to 1½ tablespoons	1⅓ to 2 tablespoons
Soft butter	⅔ teaspoon	1 teaspoon	1⅓ teaspoons

***Note:** When a recipe calls for a specific proportion of an egg (e.g., 2/3 or 1/2), you can simply beat the egg lightly and use the indicated amount of the beaten mixture. Careful measuring is recommended to ensure the best results.*

Directions:

- Following the manufacturer's instructions, add all dough ingredients to the bread machine pan except the raisins, lemon peel, and pecans. Set the crust to medium and select the Sweet Bread cycle. For this recipe, do not use the Delay Timer function.

- Toss the raisins, lemon peel, and pecan bits with 1 tablespoon of all-purpose flour while the dough kneads. This will keep them from sinking to the bottom of the oven during baking.

- Add the floured raisins, lemon peel, and pecans to the dough at the proper time (typically between Knead 1 and Knead 2) or as your machine instructs. The dough may appear dry at first, but it will level out over time, taking around 7 minutes to fully smooth out.

- Prepare the lemon icing while the bread machine finishes baking. Whisk together the confectioners' sugar, lemon zest, lemon juice or syrup, warm milk, and soft butter inside a small mixing dish. Adjust the amount of milk to reach the desired icing consistency (thick but pourable).

- When the baking cycle is finished, remove the bread from the machine and set it on a wire rack lined with parchment paper or a plate.

- Drizzle the prepared lemon icing over the top of the bread in a back-and-forth motion using a large spoon.

- As the icing cools, it will harden, forming a lovely coating over the bread.

5.1. Rosemary Bread

PREP: 20 MINUTES | COOKE: 2 HOURS

SERVING:1 LB. 8 SLICES|1,5 LBS. 12 SLICES| 2 LBS. 16 SLICES

PER SERVING: CALORIES 142 | TOTAL FAT 3G | PROTEIN 4G | CARBS 25G

Ingredient	1 Lb.	1.5 Lbs.	2 Lbs.
o Water at 80 degrees F	½ cup + 2 tablespoons	¾ cup + 1 tablespoon	1 cup
o Melted butter, cooled	1 tablespoon + 1 teaspoon	1⅔ tablespoons	2 tablespoons + 2 teaspoons
o Sugar	1⅓ teaspoons	2 teaspoons	2⅔ teaspoons
o Salt	⅔ teaspoon	1 teaspoon	1⅓ teaspoons
o Fresh rosemary, chopped	1⅓ tablespoons	2 tablespoons	2⅔ tablespoons
o White bread flour	2 cups	3 cups	4 cups
o Instant yeast	⅞ teaspoon	1⅓ teaspoons	1¾ teaspoons

Directions:

- Add all of the ingredients to your bread maker and carefully follow the manufacturer's directions.
- Set your bread machine's program to Basic/White Bread and the crust type to Medium.
- START the program.
- Wait till the cycle is finished.
- When the loaf is done, remove it from the bucket and set it aside for 5 minutes to cool.
- Shake the bucket gently to dislodge the loaves.
- Transfer to a cooling rack to cool before slicing and serving.

PREP.: 20 MINUTES | COOK: 3 HOURS 20 MINUTES

SERVING:1 LB. 8-10 SLICES|1,5 LBS. 12-15 SLICES| 2 LBS. 16-20 SLICES

PER SERVING: CALORIES 281 | TOTAL FAT 4G | PROTEIN 8G | CARBS 54G

Ingredient	1 Lb.	1.5 Lbs.	2 Lbs.
o Tomato paste	1 tablespoon + 2 teaspoons	2 tablespoons + 2 teaspoons	3 tablespoons
o Water	1 cup	1¼ cups	1½ cups
o Flour, sieved	2⅞ cups	3⅓ cups	4⅓ cups
o Vegetable oil	1 tablespoon	1 tablespoon + 1 teaspoon	1½ tablespoons
o Sugar	1⅓ teaspoons	1½ teaspoons	2 teaspoons
o Salt	1⅓ teaspoons	1½ teaspoons	2 teaspoons
o Dry yeast	1 teaspoon	1¼ teaspoons	1½ teaspoons
o Oregano, dried	⅓ teaspoon	⅓ teaspoon + a pinch	½ teaspoon
o Ground sweet paprika	⅓ teaspoon	⅓ teaspoon + a pinch	½ teaspoon

Directions:

- Dissolve the tomato paste in warm water. Adjust tomato paste to your taste, but don't use less than 1 tablespoon to maintain the bread's color.
- Make the spices. To the oregano and paprika, add a little extra oregano as well as Provencal herbs (this bread begs for spices).
- To add oxygen to the flour, sieve it. Mix in the spices with the flour.
- Add the vegetable oil inside the bread maker container. Add the tomato/water mixture, sugar, salt, flour with spices, and yeast last.
- Turn on the bread machine (the Basic program - WHITE BREAD - Medium crust).
- Turn off the bread maker once the baking cycle has finished. Take the baked bread out of the bread container. Place it on the cooling rack for 10 to 15 minutes to cool.
- Serve and enjoy.

Note: Monitor the dough during processing. If too dry, add water a teaspoon at a time. If too wet, supplement with a little flour. The goal is a smooth, nonstick dough. Adjustments may depend on the moisture or flour used.

PREP: 15 MINUTES | COOK: 3 HOURS

SERVING:1 LB. 8-10 SLICES|1,5 LBS. 12-15 SLICES| 2 LBS. 16-20 SLICES

PER SERVING: CALORIES 150 | TOTAL FAT 2G | PROTEIN 4G | CARBS 29G

Ingredient	1 Lb.	1.5 Lbs.	2 Lbs.
o Water at 80 degrees F	⅔ cup	1 cup	1 cup
o Olive brine	⅓ cup	⅓ cup + 2 tablespoons	½ cup
o Butter	1 tablespoon	1 tablespoon + 1 teaspoon	1½ tablespoons
o Sugar	2 tablespoons	2 tablespoons + 2 teaspoons	3 tablespoons
o Salt	1⅓ teaspoons	1½ teaspoons	2 teaspoons
o Flour	3⅝ cups	4½ cups	5⅓ cups
o Bread machine yeast	1⅓ teaspoons	1½ teaspoons	2 teaspoons
o Olives, black/green	13 olives	17 olives	20 olives
o Italian herbs	1 teaspoon	1⅓ teaspoons	1½ teaspoons

Directions:

- Cut the olives into slices.
- Place all ingredients (except the olives) in your bread machine and process according to the manufacturer's directions.
- Set your bread machine's program to French bread and the crust type to Medium.
- When the maker beeps, add the olives.
- Wait till the cycle is finished.
- When the loaf is done, remove it from the pan and set it aside for 6 minutes to cool.
- To remove the bread, wiggle the bucket.
- Cool for some time, then serve and enjoy.

Type of olives: Although the recipe mentions "black/green olives," it would be better to specify whether they should be boneless or not.

Type of flour: "Flour" is a generic term. For bread, it might be helpful to specify whether it is bread flour, whole wheat flour, or other type.

PREP.: 15 MINUTES | COOK: 3 HOURS

SERVING: 1 LB. 8-10 SLICES | 1,5 LBS. 12-15 SLICES | 2 LBS. 16-20 SLICES

PER SERVING: CALORIES 205 | TOTAL FAT 11G | PROTEIN 4G | CARBS 32G

Ingredient	1 Lb.	1.5 Lbs.	2 Lbs.
o Water	⅔ cup	⅚ cup	1 cup
o Active dry yeast	1⅓ teaspoons	1⅔ teaspoons	2 teaspoons
o Grated carrot	⅔ cup	⅚ cup	1 cup
o Bread flour	2⅔ cups	3⅓ cups	4 cups
o Margarine	1⅓ tablespoons	1⅔ tablespoons	2 tablespoons
o Salt	⅓ tablespoon	⅓ tablespoon + a pinch	½ tablespoon
o Sugar	1⅓ tablespoons	1⅔ tablespoons	2 tablespoons

Directions:

- Place everything in the bread machine's pan.
- Select white bread and press the start button.
- Once done baking, remove the pan from the bread maker and put aside for 10 minutes to cool.
- Serve and enjoy.

PREP.: 10 MINUTES | COOK: 3 HOURS

SERVING: 1 LB. 12 SLICES | 1,5 LBS. 18 SLICES | 2 LBS. 24 SLICES

PER SERVING: CALORIES 315 | TOTAL FAT 4G | PROTEIN 5G | CARBS 55G

Ingredient	1 Lb.	1.5 Lbs.	2 Lbs.
o Bread Flour	2¾ cups	4⅛ cups	5½ cups
o Dried fruits	1½ cups	2¼ cups	3 cups
o Sugar	4 tablespoons	6 tablespoons	8 tablespoons
o Butter	2½ tablespoons	3¾ tablespoons	5 tablespoons
o Milk powder	1 tablespoon	1½ tablespoons	2 tablespoons
o Cinnamon	1 teaspoon	1½ teaspoons	2 teaspoons
o Ground nutmeg	½ teaspoon	¾ teaspoon	1 teaspoon
o Vanilla	¼ teaspoon	⅜ teaspoon	½ teaspoon
o Peanuts	½ cup	¾ cup	1 cup
o Powdered sugar (for dusting)	As needed	As needed	As needed

Directions:

- Add all ingredients (except the peanuts and powdered sugar) to your bread machine, following the manufacturer's instructions.
- Choose the Basic/White Bread program with a Medium crust setting.
- When the bread machine prompts, moisten the dough with water and add the peanuts.
- Once the cycle is complete, remove the loaf and let it cool for 5 minutes.
- Shake the bucket gently to release the loaf.
- Dust with powdered sugar, slice, and serve.

Note: Add peanuts when the machine beeps for extra ingredients. If you miss that signal, insert them 5-10 minutes before the end of the dough. Use unsalted peanuts.

PREP.: 15 MINUTES | COOK: 2 HOURS

SERVING:1 LB. 6 SLICES|1,5 LBS. 8 SLICES| 2 LBS. 12 SLICES

PER SERVING: CALORIES 141 | TOTAL FAT 2G | PROTEIN 4G | CARBS 27G

Ingredient	1 Lb.	1.5 Lbs.	2 Lbs.
Water (80°F to 90°F)	½ cup	¾ cup	1 cup
Melted butter, cooled	2/3 tablespoon	1 tablespoon	1⅓ tablespoons
Tomato paste	1⅓ teaspoons	2 teaspoons	2⅔ teaspoons
Sugar	⅔ tablespoon	1 tablespoon	1⅓ tablespoons
Salt	⅔ teaspoon	1 teaspoon	1⅓ teaspoons
Skim milk powder	1⅓ tablespoons	2 tablespoons	2⅔ tablespoons
Cajun seasoning	⅓ tablespoon	½ tablespoon	⅔ tablespoon
Onion powder	1/12 teaspoon	⅛ teaspoon	1/6 teaspoon
White bread flour	2 cups	3 cups	4 cups
Bread machine or instant yeast	⅔ teaspoon	1 teaspoon	1⅓ teaspoons

Directions:

- Place the ingredients in your bread maker according to the manufacturer's instructions.
- Set the machine to Basic/White bread, choose the light or medium crust, and click the Start button.
- When the bread is done, allow it to sit in the machine for 5 minutes to cool.
- Afterwards, remove the bucket, gently shake it to release the loaf, then transfer the bread to a cooling rack for further cooling.
- Once cooled, slice, serve and enjoy.

Note: The Cajun seasoning and onion powder add a distinctive flavor to this bread. Depending on personal preference, you can adjust the amount of these spices to suit your taste.

5.7. Onion Bread

PREP.: 10 MINUTES | COOK: 3 HOURS

SERVING:1 LB. 6 SLICES|1,5 LBS. 8 SLICES| 2 LBS. 12 SLICES

PER SERVING: CALORIES 130 | TOTAL FAT 5G | PROTEIN 8G | CARBS 19G

Ingredient	1 Lb.	1.5 Lbs.	2 Lbs.
o *Butter*	1 tablespoon + 1 teaspoon	2 tablespoons	2 tablespoons + 2 teaspoons
o *Water*	1 cup	1 1/4 cups	1 1/2 cups
o *Sugar*	2/3 tablespoon	1 tablespoon	1 tablespoon + 1 1/2 teaspoons
o *Salt*	1 teaspoon	1 1/4 teaspoons	1 1/2 teaspoons
o *Non-fat dry milk*	1 tablespoon + 1 teaspoon	2 tablespoons	2 tablespoons + 2 teaspoons
o *Bread flour*	2 2/3 cups	3 1/3 cups	4 cups
o *Dry onion soup mix*	2 tablespoons	2 1/2 tablespoons	3 tablespoons
o *Active dry yeast*	1 1/3 teaspoons	1 2/3 teaspoons	2 teaspoons

Directions:

- Place all ingredients except the dry onion soup mix into the bread machine pan.
- Start the bread machine using the white bread cycle and medium crust option.
- Approximately 30 minutes into the cycle or when your machine signals for additional ingredients, add the dry onion soup mix.
- Once the cycle is complete, carefully remove the bread from the pan and allow it to cool for another 10 minutes on a cooling rack.
- After cooling, slice, serve, and enjoy.

Note: The onion soup mix gives the bread a unique and savory flavor, but if you prefer a milder taste, consider reducing the quantity slightly.

PREP.: 10 MINUTES | COOK: 3 HOURS

SERVING:1 LB. 6-8SLICES|1,5 LBS. 10-12 SLICES| 2 LBS. 12-16 SLICES

PER SERVING: CALORIES 129 | TOTAL FAT 3G | PROTEIN 2G | CARBS 24G

Ingredient	1 Lb.	1.5 Lbs.	2 Lbs.
o Dried yeast	1/2 teaspoon	3/4 teaspoon	1 teaspoon
o Strong white flour	2 cups	3 cups	4 cups
o Turmeric powder	1/2 teaspoon	3/4 teaspoon	1 teaspoon
o Beetroot powder	1 teaspoon	1 1/2 teaspoons	2 teaspoons
o Olive oil	1 tablespoon	1 1/2 tablespoons	2 tablespoons
o Salt	3/4 teaspoon	1 1/8 teaspoons	1 1/2 teaspoons
o Chili flakes	1/2 teaspoon	3/4 teaspoon	1 teaspoon
o Water	3/4 cup minus 1tbsp	1 1/16 cups	1 3/8 cups

Directions:

- Add each ingredient to the bread machine in the sequence and at the temperature indicated by the maker of your bread machine.
- Close the cover and start your bread maker with the basic bread, medium crust option.
- Remove the bread from the bread maker and place it on a cooling rack to cool.
- Serve and enjoy.

PREP: 10 MINUTES | COOK 3 HOURS 25 MINUTES

SERVING:1 LB. 6-8SLICES|1,5 LBS. 10-12 SLICES| 2 LBS. 12-16 SLICES

PER SERVING: CALORIES 276 | TOTAL FAT 3G | PROTEIN 8G | CARBS 54G

Ingredient	1 Lb.	1.5 Lbs.	2 Lbs.
o Wheat flour	2 cups	3 cups	4 cups
o Sugar	1/2 tablespoon	3/4 tablespoon	1 tablespoon
o Sunflower oil	1/2 tablespoon	3/4 tablespoon	1 tablespoon
o Salt	3/4 teaspoon	1 1/8 teaspoons	1 1/2 teaspoons
o Water	3/4 cup	1 1/8 cups	1 1/2 cups
o Dry yeast	1/2 teaspoon	3/4 teaspoon	1 teaspoon
o Mashed potatoes (sieved)	1/2 cup	3/4 cup	1 cup
o Crushed rosemary	*To taste	*To taste	*To taste

*To taste (adjust proportionally)

Directions:

- In the bread maker bucket, add the flour, salt, and sugar.
- Next, pour in the sunflower oil and water.
- Make sure the salt and yeast do not come in direct contact, and then add the yeast to the mixture.
- Set your bread machine to the Bread with a Filling setting and the crust type to Medium.
- When prompted, open the top and add the mashed potatoes and rosemary.
- Once the cycle is finished, remove the loaf from the bucket and allow it to cool for 5 minutes.
- Shake the bucket gently to release the loaf.
- Serve and enjoy.

PREP.: 10 MINUTES | COOK: 3 HOURS 25 MINUTES

SERVING:1 LB. 6-8SLICES|1,5 LBS. 10-12 SLICES| 2 LBS. 12-16 SLICES

PER SERVING: CALORIES 226 | TOTAL FAT 2G | PROTEIN 7G | CARBS 46G

Ingredient	1 Lb.	1.5 Lbs.	2 Lbs.
o Wheat flour	3/4 cup	1 1/8 cups	1½ cups
o Whole-meal flour	1 1/6 cups	1¾ cups	2 1/3 cups
o Fresh yeast	1/2 teaspoon	3/4 teaspoon	1 teaspoon
o Water	3/4 cup	1 1/8 cups	1½ cups
o Culinary-grade Lavender.	1/2 teaspoon	3/4 teaspoon	1 teaspoon
o Honey	3/4 tablespoon	1 tablespoon + 1/4 tablespoon	1½ tablespoons
o Salt	1/2 teaspoon	3/4 teaspoon	1 teaspoon

Directions:

- Sift both types of flour into a mixing bowl and combine.
- Add water, honey, and lavender to your bread machine pan.
- Ensure that the salt and yeast do not come into direct contact, then add the salt and yeast.
- Carefully follow the manufacturer's directions for your bread machine.
- Set your bread machine program to Basic/White Bread and select the Medium crust option.
- Wait until the cycle is completed.
- Once the loaf is done, remove it from the pan and allow it to cool for 5 minutes.
- Gently shake the pan to dislodge the loaf.
- Serve and enjoy.

6.1. Cheesy Garlic Bread

PREP.: 10 MINUTES | COOK: 1 HOUR 30 MINUTES

SERVING:1 LB. 8SLICES|1,5 LBS. 12 SLICES| 2 LBS. 16 SLICES

PER SERVING: CALORIES 129 | TOTAL FAT 9G | PROTEIN 2G | CARBS 11G

Ingredient	1 Lb.	1.5 Lbs.	2 Lbs.
o Mozzarella, shredded	3/4 cup	1 1/8 cups	1 1/2 cups
o Almond flour	1 1/2 cups	2 1/4 cups	3 cups
o Cream cheese	2 tablespoons	3 tablespoons	4 tablespoons
o Garlic, crushed	1 tablespoon	1 1/2 tablespoons	2 tablespoons
o Parsley (bread)	1 tablespoon	1 1/2 tablespoons	2 tablespoons
o Baking powder	1 teaspoon	1 1/2 teaspoons	2 teaspoons
o Salt	to taste	to taste	to taste
o Egg	1	1 (may require slight adjustment)	2

For the toppings:

	1 Lb.	1.5 Lbs.	2 Lbs.
o Melted butter	2 tablespoons	3 tablespoons	4 tablespoons
o Parsley	1/2 teaspoon	3/4 teaspoon	1 teaspoon
o Garlic clove, minced	1 teaspoon	1 1/2 teaspoons	2 teaspoons

Directions:

- Begin by adding the wet ingredients to the bread machine pan (cream cheese, garlic, egg).
- Add the dry ingredients (mozzarella, almond flour, parsley, baking powder, and salt).
- Set the bread machine to the basic bread option.
- After baking, transfer the bread to a cooling rack and allow it to cool for a few minutes.
- Drizzle the melted butter topping mixture over the bread, and sprinkle with parsley and minced garlic.
- Serve and enjoy.
-

6.2. Jalapeno Cheese Bread

PREP.: 10 MINUTES | COOK: 3 HOURS

SERVING:1 LB. 8SLICES|1,5 LBS. 12 SLICES| 2 LBS. 16 SLICES

PER SERVING: CALORIES 150 | TOTAL FAT 4G | PROTEIN 7G | CARBS 22G

Ingredient	1 Lb.	1.5 Lbs.	2 Lbs.
o Bread flour	2 cups	3 cups	4 cups
o Active dry yeast	1 teaspoon	1 1/2 teaspoons	2 teaspoons
o Water	2/3 cup	1 cup	1 1/3 cups
o Sugar	1 1/3 tablespoons	2 tablespoons	2 2/3 tablespoons
o Salt	2/3 teaspoon	1 teaspoon	1 1/3 teaspoon
o Shredded cheddar cheese	1/3 cup	1/2 cup	2/3 cup
o Diced jalapeno peppers	2 2/3 tablespoons	1/4 cup	1/3 cup

Directions:

- Add each ingredient to the bread machine in the sequence and at the temperature indicated by the maker of your bread machine.
- Close the cover and start your bread maker with the basic bread, medium crust option.
- When your bread has finished baking, remove it from the bread maker and place it on a cooling rack to cool.
- Serve and enjoy.

PREP.: 10 MINUTES | COOK: 1 HOUR 40 MINUTES

SERVING:1 LB. 8SLICES|1,5 LBS. 12 SLICES| 2 LBS. 16 SLICES

PER SERVING: CALORIES 115 | TOTAL FAT 6G | PROTEIN 8G | CARBS 33G

Ingredient	1 Lb.	1.5 Lbs.	2 Lbs.
o *Milk*	1/3 cup	1/2 cup	2/3 cup
o *Ricotta cheese*	1 cup	1 1/2 cups	2 cups
o *Butter*	2 tablespoons	3 tablespoons	4 tablespoons
o *Egg*	1 egg	1.5 eggs (1 large + 1 yolk)	2 eggs
o *Sugar*	2 ½ tablespoons	3 ¾ tablespoons	5 tablespoons
o *Salt*	1 teaspoon	1 1/2 teaspoons	2 teaspoons
o *Bread flour*	2 ¼ cups	3 3/8 cups	4 1/2 cups
o *Yeast*	1 ½ teaspoons	2 1/4 teaspoons	3 teaspoons

Directions:

- Place all bread ingredients in the bread machine in the order stated above, beginning with the milk and ending with the yeast.
- Make an indentation in the middle of the flour and place the yeast in it. Make certain that the well does not come into contact with any liquid. Set the bread machine on basic with a light crust setting.
- After around 5 minutes, check the dough to ensure it is a softball. If it's too dry, add 1 tablespoon of water at a time, and if it's too wet, add 1 tablespoon of flour.
- Allow the bread to cool on a wire rack after it has finished baking.
- Serve and enjoy.

6.4. Parmesan Italian Bread

PREP: 10 MINUTES | COOK: 2 HOURS

SERVING: 1 LB. 12 SLICES | 1,5 LBS. 16 SLICES | 2 LBS. 22 SLICES

PER SERVING: CALORIES 150 | TOTAL FAT 5G | PROTEIN 5G | CARBS 14G

Ingredient	1 Lb.	1.5 Lbs.	2 Lbs.
o *Warm water*	1 1/3 cups	2 cups	2 2/3 cups
o *Olive oil*	2 tablespoons	3 tablespoons	4 tablespoons
o *Garlic, crushed*	2 cloves	3 cloves	4 cloves
o *Basil*	1 tablespoon	1 1/2 tablespoons	2 tablespoons
o *Oregano*	1 tablespoon	1 1/2 tablespoons	2 tablespoons
o *Parsley*	1 tablespoon	1 1/2 tablespoons	2 tablespoons
o *Almond flour*	2 cups	3 cups	4 cups
o *Inulin*	1 tablespoon	1 1/2 tablespoons	2 tablespoons
o *Parmesan cheese, grated*	1/2 cup	3/4 cup	1 cup
o *Active dry yeast*	1 teaspoon	1 1/2 teaspoons	2 teaspoons

Directions:

- Add the wet ingredients (water, olive oil, and crushed garlic) to the bread machine pan.
- Add the dry ingredients (basil, oregano, parsley, almond flour, inulin, and parmesan cheese).
- Make a small well in the middle and add the active dry yeast.
- Set the bread machine to French bread mode.
- Once baked, transfer the bread to a cooling rack.
- Serve and enjoy.
- Note: This bread is gluten-free due to almond flour.

6.5. Cheese Blend Bread

PREP.: 10 MINUTES | COOK: 1 HOUR 30 MINUTES

SERVING:1 LB. 8 SLICES|1,5 LBS. 12 SLICES| 2 LBS. 16 SLICES

PER SERVING: CALORIES 132 | TOTAL FAT 8G | PROTEIN 6G | CARBS 16G

Ingredient	1 Lb.	1.5 Lbs.	2 Lbs.
o Cream cheese	2/3 cup	1 cup	1 1/3 cups
o Ghee	1/4 cup	3/8 cup	1/2 cup
o Almond flour	2/3 cup	1 cup	1 1/3 cups
o Coconut flour	1/4 cup	3/8 cup	1/2 cup
o Whey protein, unflavored	3 tablespoons	4.5 tablespoons	6 tablespoons
o Baking powder	2 teaspoons	3 teaspoons	4 teaspoons
o Himalayan salt	1/2 teaspoon	3/4 teaspoon	1 teaspoon
o Parmesan cheese, shredded	1/2 cup	3/4 cup	1 cup
o Water	3 tablespoons	4.5 tablespoons	6 tablespoons
o Eggs	3	5 (rounded)	6
o Mozzarella cheese, shredded	1/2 cup	3/4 cup	1 cup

Directions:

- Place the wet ingredients in the bread machine pan. Combine the dry ingredients. Set the bread machine to the gluten-free option.
- When the bread is done, take the bread machine pan out. Allow to cool slightly before transferring to a cooling rack.
- Serve and enjoy.
- Bread can be kept in the refrigerator for up to 5 days.

6.6. Bell Pepper Cheddar Bread

PREP.: 10 MINUTES | COOK: 1 HOUR 30 MINUTES

SERVING:1 LB. 8 SLICES|1,5 LBS. 12 SLICES| 2 LBS. 16 SLICES

PER SERVING: CALORIES 165 | TOTAL FAT 5G | PROTEIN 5G | CARBS 25G

Ingredient	1 Lb.	1.5 Lbs.	2 Lbs.
o Lukewarm buttermilk	1 cup	1 1/2 cups	2 cups
o Unsalted and melted butter	1/4 cup	3/8 cup	1/2 cup
o Eggs at room temperature	2	3	4
o Table salt	1/2 teaspoon	3/4 teaspoon	1 teaspoon
o Bell pepper, chopped	1	1.5 (rounded)	2
o Cheddar cheese, shredded	1/2 cup	3/4 cup	1 cup
o Sugar	1/4 cup	3/8 cup	1/2 cup
o All-purpose flour	1 1/3 cups	2 cups	2 2/3 cups
o Cornmeal	1 cup	1 1/2 cups	2 cups
o Baking powder	1 tablespoon	1.5 tablespoons	2 tablespoons

Directions:

- Prepare the ingredients.
- Determine the size of the loaf you want to create and measure your ingredients.
- In the sequence listed above, add the ingredients to the bread pan.
- Close the lid on the bread maker and place the pan inside.
- Start the bread machine. Choose the Rapid/Quick setting, then the loaf size, and finally, the color of the crust. Begin the cycle.
- When the cycle is complete, and the bread is baked, carefully remove the pan from the machine. Because the handle will be quite hot, use a potholder. Allow for a few minutes of rest.
- Remove the bread from the pan and cool for at least 10 minutes on a wire rack before slicing.

Note: Before using Rapid/Quick mode, we recommend that you consult your bread machine manual to make sure the settings are optimal for this recipe. Each model may have slight variations in settings.

6.7. Roasted Garlic Asiago Bread

PREP.: 10 MINUTES | COOK: 1 HOUR

SERVING:1 LB. 8 SLICES|1,5 LBS. 12 SLICES| 2 LBS. 16 SLICES

PER SERVING: CALORIES 188 | TOTAL FAT 6G | PROTEIN 5G | CARBS 28G

Ingredient	1 Lb.	1.5 Lbs.	2 Lbs.
o milk, at 70°F to 80°F	1/2 cup + 2 teaspoons	3/4 cup + 1 tablespoon	1 cup
o melted butter, cooled	2 2/3 tablespoons	1/4 cup	1/3 cup
o minced garlic	2/3 teaspoon	1 teaspoon	1 1/3 teaspoon
o Sugar	1 1/3 tablespoons	2 tablespoons	2 2/3 tablespoons
o salt	2/3 teaspoon	1 teaspoon	1 1/3 teaspoon
o grated Asiago cheese	1/3 cup	1/2 cup	2/3 cup
o white bread flour	1 5/6 cups	2 3/4 cups	3 2/3 cups
o Bread machine or instant yeast	1 teaspoon	1 1/2 teaspoons	2 teaspoons
o mashed roasted garlic	1/3 cup	1/2 cup	2/3 cup

Directions:

- Prepare the ingredients.
- Place all of the ingredients, except the roasted garlic, in the bread machine according to the manufacturer's instructions.
- Set the machine to Basic/White bread, choose the light or medium crust, and click the Start button.
- When the bread machine beeps, or 5 minutes before the last kneading, add the roasted garlic.
- Shake the bucket gently to remove the loaf and place it on a cooling rack to cool.
- Remove the bucket from the machine when the bread is finished.
- Allow the bread to cool for 5 minutes before slicing.

6.8. Cottage Cheese and Chive Bread

PREP.: 10 MINUTES | COOK: 1 HOUR

SERVING:1 LB. 8 SLICES|1,5 LBS. 12 SLICES| 2 LBS. 16 SLICES

PER SERVING: CALORIES 173 | TOTAL FAT 4G | PROTEIN 7G | CARBS 29G

Ingredient	1 Lb.	1.5 Lbs.	2 Lbs.
o water	1/4 cup	5/16 cup	3/8 cup
o cottage cheese	2/3 cup	5/6 cup	1 cup
o large egg	1 small egg	1 medium egg	1 large egg
o butter	1 1/3 tablespoons	1 2/3 tablespoons	2 tablespoons
o salt	1 teaspoon	1 1/4 teaspoons	1 1/2 teaspoons
o white bread flour	2 1/2 cups	3 1/8 cups	3 3/4 cups
o dried chives	2 tablespoons	2 1/2 tablespoons	3 tablespoons
o granulated sugar	1 2/3 tablespoons	2 1/6 tablespoons	2 1/2 tablespoons
o active dry yeast	1 1/2 teaspoons	2 teaspoons	2 1/4 teaspoons

Directions:

- Assemble the ingredients.
- Add each ingredient to the bread machine in the sequence and at the temperature indicated by the maker of your bread machine.
- Close the cover and start your bread maker with the basic bread, medium crust option.
- Remove the bread from the bread maker and place it on a cooling rack to cool.

Note on Baking: It is recommended that you consult your bread machine manual to ensure that the settings are optimal for this particular recipe.

6.9. Beer and Cheese Bread

PREP.: 10 MINUTES | COOK: 1 HOUR

SERVING:1 LB. 8 SLICES|1,5 LBS. 12 SLICES| 2 LBS. 16 SLICES

PER SERVING: CALORIES 174 | TOTAL FAT 3G | PROTEIN 5G | CARBS 31G

Ingredient	1 Lb.	1.5 Lbs.	2 Lbs.
o bread or all-purpose flour	2 cups	2 1/2 cups	3 cups
o instant yeast	2/3 tablespoon	1 tablespoon	1 1/3 tablespoons
o salt	2/3 teaspoon	3/4 teaspoon	1 teaspoon
o sugar	2/3 tablespoon	3/4 tablespoon	1 tablespoon
o beer at room temperature	1 cup	1 1/4 cups	1 1/2 cups
o shredded Monterey cheese	1/3 cup	approx. 1/2 cup minus 1 tbsp	1/2 cup
o shredded Edam cheese	1/3 cup	approx. 1/2 cup minus 1 tbsp	1/2 cup

Directions:

- In the bread pan, stack all ingredients except the cheeses in the liquid-dry-yeast layering.
- Place the pan in the bread maker.
- Choose the Bake cycle. Select the Regular Basic Setting. Press the start.
- When the bread machine beeps, add the cheese.
- Wait until the loaf has finished cooking.
- After the bread is finished, the machine will enter the keep warm mode.
- Remember to leave it in that mode for around 10 minutes before unplugging it.
- Finally, remove the pan and set it aside to cool for about 10 minutes before serving.

6.10. Cheese Swirl Loaf

PREP.: 10 MINUTES | COOK: 1 HOUR

SERVING:1 LB. 12 SLICES|1,5 LBS. 18 SLICES| 2 LBS. 24 SLICES

PER SERVING: CALORIES 211 | TOTAL FAT 9G | PROTEIN 7G | CARBS 32G

Ingredient	1 Lb.	1.5 Lbs.	2 Lbs.
o all-purpose flour	2 cups	2 1/2 cups	3 cups
o lukewarm milk	5/6 cup (approx. 3/4 cup + 2 tbsp)	1 cup + 1/8 cup	1 1/4 cups
o sugar	2/3 tablespoon	1 tablespoon	1 1/3 tablespoons
o salt	2/3 teaspoon	3/4 teaspoon	1 teaspoon
o instant yeast	1 teaspoon	1 1/4 teaspoons	1 1/2 teaspoons
o melted butter	1 1/3 tablespoons	1 2/3 tablespoons	2 tablespoons
o slices of Monterey cheese	3	3.5 (3 slices and half of another)	4
o mozzarella cheese	1/3 cup	approx. 1/2 cup minus 1 tbsp	1/2 cup
o edam or any quick melting cheese	1/3 cup	approx. 1/2 cup minus 1 tbsp	1/2 cup
o paprika	1/3 teaspoon	7/12 teaspoon approx. a bit over 1/2 tsp)	1/2 teaspoon

. Directions:

- In the bread pan, add all ingredients except the cheeses in the liquid-dry-yeast layering.
- Place the pan in the bread maker.
- Select the Bake cycle. Select the Regular Basic Setting option. Press the start.
- When the bread machine beeps, melt all the cheese in a microwave-safe bowl for 30 seconds. Keep cool but soft. Spread the cheese on the top of the loaf.
- Continue to wait until the loaf is done.
- When the bread is finished, the machine will enter the keep warm mode.
- Allow it to stay in that mode for about 10 minutes before unplugging it.
- Finally, remove the pan and set it aside for about 10 minutes to cool before serving.

Note: Quantities may require minor adjustments based on taste preference and desired consistency.

CHAPTER 7: Quick Bread Recipes

7.1. Zucchini Rye Bread

PREP.: 10 MINUTES | COOK: 25 MINUTES

SERVING:1 LB. 8 SLICES|1,5 LBS. 12 SLICES| 2 LBS. 16 SLICES

PER SERVING: CALORIES 277 | TOTAL FAT 7G | PROTEIN 9G | CARBS 48G

Ingredient	1 Lb.	1.5 Lbs.	2 Lbs.
o all-purpose or bread flour	1 cup	1 1/2 cups	2 cups
o rye flour	1 1/2 cups	2 1/8 cups	2 3/4 cups
o cocoa powder	1 tablespoon	1 1/2 tablespoons	2 tablespoons
o cornmeal	1/3 cup	1/4 cup + 2 tablespoons	1/2 cup
o baking powder	2/3 tablespoon	1 tablespoon	1 1/3 tablespoons
o baking soda	1/3 teaspoon	1/2 teaspoon	1/2 teaspoon
o olive oil	2 tablespoons + 2 teaspoons	3 tablespoons + 1 1/2 teaspoon	1/4 cup
o molasses or honey	2 tablespoons	2 1/2 tablespoons	3 tablespoons
o lukewarm water	1 cup	1 1/4 cups	1 1/2 cups
o salt	2/3 teaspoon	3/4 teaspoon	1 teaspoon
o zucchini, shredded	1 cup	1 1/4 cups	1 1/2 cups

Directions:

- Wring out shredded zucchini using a towel to remove excess moisture.
- Add ingredients to the bread machine in the order recommended by the manufacturer, typically starting with wet ingredients followed by dry.
- Choose the "Bake" cycle and select the "Quick/Rapid" setting with a medium crust.
- Once baked, let the bread remain in the machine's "keep warm" mode for about ten minutes before unplugging.
- Remove the bread pan and let it cool for an additional 10 minutes before serving.

Note: The cocoa powder in the recipe gives the bread a darker hue but doesn't significantly influence the taste towards a chocolate flavor.

PREP.: 20 MINUTES | COOK: 40 MINUTES

SERVING:1 LB. 8 SLICES|1,5 LBS. 12 SLICES| 2 LBS. 16 SLICES

PER SERVING: CALORIES 310 | TOTAL FAT 13G | PROTEIN 3G | CARBS 40G

Ingredient	1 Lb.	1.5 Lbs.	2 Lbs.
o Baking Powder	1 teaspoon	1 1/2 teaspoons	2 teaspoons
o Baking Soda	1/2 teaspoon	3/4 teaspoon	1 teaspoon
o Bananas, Peeled and Halved Lengthwise	2 bananas	3 bananas	4 bananas
o All-Purpose Flour	2 cups	3 cups	4 cups
o Eggs	2 eggs	3 eggs	4 eggs
o Vegetable Oil	3 tablespoons	4 1/2 tablespoons	6 tablespoons
o White Sugar	3/4 cup	1 1/8 cups	1 1/2 cups

Directions:

- Mash the bananas in a bowl until they form a smooth paste.
- Place all of the ingredients, including the mashed bananas, in the bread pan and select the dough setting. Begin by mixing for around 3-5 minutes.
- After 3-5 minutes, push the stop button. Smooth the dough's surface using the spatula, select the Quick/Rapid setting, start, and bake for 35 minutes. Check for doneness by inserting a toothpick into the top center. If it comes out clean, the bread is done.
- When the bread is finished baking, take it from the machine and let it in the pan for 10 minutes. Remove the bread and place it on a wire rack to cool.
- Serve and enjoy.

Note: Quantities may require minor adjustments based on taste preference and desired consistency.

7.3. Dried Cranberry Tea Bread

PREP.: 20 MINUTES | COOK: 40 MINUTES

SERVING:1 LB. 8 SLICES|1,5 LBS. 12 SLICES| 2 LBS. 16 SLICES

PER SERVING: CALORIES 333 | TOTAL FAT 14G | PROTEIN 5G | CARBS 37G

Ingredient	1 Lb.	1.5 Lbs.	2 Lbs.
o Dried Cranberries	1 cup	1½ cups	2 cups
o Boiling Water	Adequate to cover	Adequate to cover	Adequate to cover
o Large Eggs	1 egg	2 eggs	3 eggs
o Almond Extract	1 1/3 teaspoons	2 teaspoons	2 2/3 teaspoons
o Vanilla Extract	2/3 teaspoon	1 teaspoon	1 1/3 teaspoons
o Canola Or Vegetable Oil	2/3 cup	1 cup	1 1/3 cup
o Unsweetened Apple Juice Concentrate, Thawed	1/2 cup	¾ cup	1 cup
o Sugar	2/3 cup	1 cup	1 1/3 cups
o Whole Wheat Pastry Flour	2/3 cup	1 cup	1 1/3 cups
o Unbleached All-Purpose Flour	5/6 cup	1¼ cups	1 2/3 cups
o Baking Soda	1/3 teaspoon	½ teaspoon	2/3 teaspoon
o Baking Powder	2/3 tablespoon	1 tablespoon	1 1/3 tablespoons
o Ground Cinnamon	2/3 teaspoon	1 teaspoon	1 1/3 teaspoons
o Fresh-Ground Nutmeg	1/3 teaspoon	½ teaspoon	2/3 teaspoon
o Salt	1/3 teaspoon	½ teaspoon	2/3 teaspoon

Directions:

- In a small bowl, cover cranberries with boiling water, letting them soften for 20 minutes. Drain well and pat dry with paper towels. Set it aside.
- Add ingredients to the bread machine in the order specified by the manufacturer, typically wet ingredients followed by dry, then cranberries.
- If available, select the dark crust setting. Then choose the "Quick Bread/Cake" cycle and start.
- Once the cycle ends, check doneness using a toothpick or skewer. The bread should have dark brown sides, a firm top, and the toothpick should come out clean. If it's still wet, consider running a second cycle or baking for a few additional minutes.
- Once baked, remove from the machine and cool in the pan for 10 minutes. Turn out onto a rack to cool completely.

PREP.: 20 MINUTES | COOK: 30 MINUTES

SERVING:1 LB. 8 SLICES|1,5 LBS. 12 SLICES| 2 LBS. 16 SLICES

PER SERVING: CALORIES 277 | TOTAL FAT 11G | PROTEIN 9G | CARBS 48G

Ingredient	1 Lb.	1.5 Lbs.	2 Lbs.
o Milk (80°F to 90°F)	1/3 cup	1/2 cup	2/3 cup
o Melted butter, cooled	2 tablespoons	3 tablespoons	4 tablespoons
o Sugar	2 tablespoons	3 tablespoons	4 tablespoons
o Salt	1 teaspoon	1½ teaspoons	2 teaspoons
o Sliced fresh strawberries	1/2 cup	¾ cup	1 cup
o Quick oats	2/3 cup	1 cup	1 1/3 cups
o White bread flour	1 1/2 cups	2¼ cups	3 cups
o Baking powder	2/3 tablespoon	1 tablespoon	1 1/3 tablespoons
o Baking soda	1/3 teaspoon	½ teaspoon	2/3 teaspoon

Directions:

- Ensure strawberries are washed, hulled, and dried properly before slicing.
- Add ingredients to the bread machine in the order recommended by the manufacturer.
- Select the "Bake" cycle and the "Quick" setting. Choose either light or medium crust.
- Once baked, remove the bread pan and cool for 5 minutes. Gently release the loaf and transfer to a cooling rack.
- Allow to cool completely before slicing. Serving while slightly warm is recommended for the best flavor and texture.

Note: *Quantities may require minor adjustments based on taste preference and desired consistency. As always, I recommend that you monitor the consistency of the dough during preparation, as you may need to make minor adjustments depending on your bread machine.*

7.5. Cloud Savory Bread Loaf

PREP.: 10 MINUTES | COOK: 20 MINUTES

SERVING:1 LB. 12 SLICES|1,5 LBS. 18 SLICES| 2 LBS. 24 SLICES

PER SERVING: CALORIES 90 | TOTAL FAT 7G | PROTEIN 6G | CARBS 8G

Ingredient	1 Lb.	1.5 Lbs.	2 Lbs.
o Egg yolks	6	9	12
o Egg whites	6	9	12
o Whey protein powder, unflavored	1/2 cup	3/4 cup	1 cup
o Cream of tartar	1/2 teaspoon	3/4 teaspoon	1 teaspoon
o Sour cream	3/4 cup	1 1/8 cups	1 1/2 cups
o Baking powder	1/2 teaspoon	3/4 teaspoon	1 teaspoon
o Garlic powder	1/4 teaspoon	3/8 teaspoon	1/2 teaspoon
o Onion powder	1/4 teaspoon	3/8 teaspoon	1/2 teaspoon
o Salt	1/4 teaspoon	3/8 teaspoon	1/2 teaspoon

Directions:

- Whisk the cream of tartar & egg whites until stiff peaks form. Set aside.
- In a different bowl, combine the rest of the ingredients.
- Gently fold the egg whites into the yolk mixture, a bit at a time, taking care not to deflate the egg whites too much.
- Pour mixture into the bread machine pan.
- Select the "Quick bread" setting on the bread machine.
- Once baked, remove the bread pan and allow the loaf to cool slightly before transferring to a cooling rack. Allow to cool for at least half an hour before slicing. This ensures the bread retains its fluffy texture.
- Bread can be stored at room temperature for up to 3 days.

Note: *Quantities may require minor adjustments based on taste preference and desired consistency. As always, I recommend that you monitor the consistency of the dough during preparation, as you may need to make minor adjustments depending on your bread machine.*

PREP TIME: 10 MINUTES | COOK TIME: 25 MINUTES

SERVING:1 LB. 8 SLICES|1,5 LBS. 12 SLICES| 2 LBS. 16 SLICES

PER SERVING: CALORIES 319 | TOTAL FAT 6G | PROTEIN 10G | CARBS 29G

Ingredient	1 Lb.	1.5 Lbs.	2 Lbs.
o Baking powder	1 tablespoon	1 1/2 tablespoons	2 tablespoons
o Active dry yeast	1 packet	1 1/2 packets	2 packets
o Baking soda	1/2 teaspoon	3/4 teaspoon	1 teaspoon
o White bread flour	2 cups	3 cups	4 cups
o Salt	1 tablespoon	1 1/2 tablespoons	2 tablespoons
o Sugar	1 1/2 tablespoons	2 1/4 tablespoons	3 tablespoons
o Water	7/8 cup	1 1/3 cups	1 3/4 cups
o Topping (olive oil, sesame seeds, poppy seeds, or cornmeal)	As needed	As needed	As needed

Directions:

- In the bread machine, combine flour, salt, sugar, baking powder, baking soda, and water in the sequence recommended by the manufacturer.
- Select the Quick bread option and the light crust.
- After baking, let the bread cool for 5 minutes before taking out of the pan. Place the bread on a cooling rack and brush the top lightly with olive oil.
- Sprinkle with poppy seeds, sesame seeds, or cornmeal. Allow to cool completely before slicing or storing.
- Store in a covered container in the freezer or at room temperature.

Note: Quantities may require minor adjustments based on taste preference and desired consistency. As always, I recommend that you monitor the consistency of the dough during preparation, as you may need to make minor adjustments depending on your bread machine.

7.7. Peaches and Butter Cream Bread

PREP.: 10 MIN. | COOK: 25 MINS.

SERVING:1 LB. 8 SLICES|1,5 LBS. 12 SLICES| 2 LBS. 16 SLICES

PER SERVING: CALORIES 277 | TOTAL FAT 4G | PROTEIN 10G | CARBS 29G

Ingredient	1 Lb.	1.5 Lbs.	2 Lbs.
o Canned peaches, drained and chopped	3/8 cup	A little more than 1/2 cup	3/4 cup
o Heavy whipping cream (80°F to 90°F)	2 tablespoons + 2 teaspoons	1/4 cup	1/3 cup
o Egg at room temperature	*1/2	*3/4	1
o Melted butter, cooled	1/2 tablespoon	3/4 tablespoon	1 tablespoon
o Sugar	1 1/8 tablespoons	1 3/4 tablespoons	2 1/4 tablespoons
o Ground cinnamon	1/6 teaspoon	1/4 teaspoon	1/3 teaspoon
o Salt	9/16 teaspoon	3/4 teaspoon	1 1/8 teaspoons
o Ground nutmeg	1/16 teaspoon	1/12 teaspoon	1/8 teaspoon
o Whole-wheat flour	1/6 cup	1/4 cup	1/3 cup
o White bread flour	1 1/3 cups	2 cups	2 2/3 cups
o Baking powder	3/4 teaspoon	1 1/8 teaspoons	1 1/2 teaspoons
o Baking soda	1/4 teaspoon	3/8 teaspoon	1/2 teaspoon

* Whisk the eggs in a cup and use the required amount.

Directions:

- In your bread maker, begin with the wet ingredients, then add the dry ones, finally adding the baking powder and soda last.
- Choose the Quick Bread setting and choose light or medium crust, then push the Start button.
- When the bread is finished, remove the bucket from the machine.
- Allow 5 minutes for the bread to cool.
- Jiggle the bucket to remove the loaf, then lay it on a rack to cool.
- Serve and enjoy.

7.8. Pineapple Coconut Bread

PREP.: 10 MINUTES | COOK: 25 MINUTES

SERVING:1 LB. 8 SLICES|1,5 LBS. 12 SLICES| 2 LBS. 16 SLICES

PER SERVING: CALORIES 238 | TOTAL FAT 4G | PROTEIN 7G | CARBS 29G

Ingredient	1 Lb.	1.5 Lbs.	2 Lbs.
o Butter at room temperature	6 tablespoons	9 tablespoons	12 tablespoons
o Eggs at room temperature	2	3	4
o Coconut milk at room temperature	1/2 cup	3/4 cup	1 cup
o Pineapple juice at room temperature	1/2 cup	3/4 cup	1 cup
o Sugar	1 cup	1 1/2 cups	2 cups
o Coconut extract	1 1/2 teaspoons	2 1/4 teaspoons	3 teaspoons
o All-purpose flour	2 cups	3 cups	4 cups
o Baking powder	1 teaspoon	1 1/2 teaspoons	2 teaspoons
o Shredded sweetened coconut	3/4 cup	1 1/8 cups	1 1/2 cups
o Salt	1/2 teaspoon	3/4 teaspoon	1 teaspoon

Directions:

- In your bread machine, combine butter, sugar, coconut milk, pineapple juice, coconut extract & eggs.
- Select the Bake cycle and set the machine to Rapid/Quick bread. In a different bowl, combine flour, coconut, baking powder, and salt. Add this dry mixture after the wet ingredients have been mixed.
- Once the bread is done, remove the pan from the machine. Allow the bread to cool for 5 minutes. Transfer the loaf to a cooling rack.
- Serve and enjoy.

Note: *Quantities may require minor adjustments based on taste preference and desired consistency. As always, I recommend that you monitor the consistency of the dough during preparation, as you may need to make minor adjustments depending on your bread machine.*

7.9. Poppy Seed Lemon Bread

PREP: 10 MIN. | COOKING TIME: 25 MIN.

SERVING:1 LB. 8 SLICES|1,5 LBS. 12 SLICES| 2 LBS. 16 SLICES

PER SERVING: CALORIES 150 | TOTAL FAT 14G | PROTEIN 3G | CARBS 19G

Ingredient	1 Lb.	1.5 Lbs.	2 Lbs.
o Water (70° to 80°)	1/2 cup	3/4 cup	1 cup
o Large egg	2/3 (use a medium egg)	1	1 1/3 (or 1 large + 1 small)
o Lemon juice	2 tablespoons	3 tablespoons	4 tablespoons
o Salt	1/2 teaspoon	3/4 teaspoon	1 teaspoon
o Bread flour	2 cups	3 cups	4 cups
o Poppy seeds	1 1/3 tablespoons	2 tablespoons	2 2/3 tablespoons
o Ground nutmeg	1/6 teaspoon	1/4 teaspoon	1/3 teaspoon
o Active dry yeast	1 1/2 teaspoons	2-1/4 teaspoons	3 teaspoons
o Melted butter	2 tablespoons	3 tablespoons	4 tablespoons
o Sugar	2 tablespoons	3 tablespoons	4 tablespoons
o Ground lemon zest	2/3 tablespoon	1 tablespoon	1 1/3 tablespoon

For the Nutmeg Butter:

	1 Lb.	1.5 Lbs.	2 Lbs.
o Butter, melted	1/3 cup	1/2 cup	2/3 cup
o Confectioners' sugar	1/3 cup	1/2 cup	2/3 cup
o Ground nutmeg	1/6 teaspoon	1/4 teaspoon	1/3 teaspoon

Directions:

- Place the first 11 ingredients specified by the maker in the bread machine container.
- Choose the Quick Bread setting and choose light or medium crust, then push the Start button.
- After 5 minutes of mixing, check the dough and add 1 to 2 tablespoons of water or flour if necessary.
- Mix the nutmeg butter ingredients in a small bowl until well combined. Refrigerate until ready to serve.
- When the bread is finished, remove the bucket from the machine.
- Serve with nutmeg butter and enjoy.

7.10. Curd Bread

PREP.: 10 MIN.| COOK: 25 MIN.

SERVING:1 LB. 8 SLICES|1,5 LBS. 12 SLICES| 2 LBS. 16 SLICES

PER SERVING: CALORIES 284 | TOTAL FAT 5G | PROTEIN 9G | CARBS 48G

Ingredient	1 Lb.	1.5 Lbs.	2 Lbs.
o Lukewarm water	1/2 cup	5/8 cup	¾ cup
o Wheat bread machine flour	2 1/4 cups	3 cups	3 2/3 cups
o Cottage cheese	1/2 cup	5/8 cup	¾ cup
o Softened butter	1 1/3 tablespoons	1 2/3 tablespoons	2 tablespoons
o White sugar	1 1/3 tablespoons	1 2/3 tablespoons	2 tablespoons
o Sea salt	1 teaspoon	1 1/4 teaspoons	1 ½ teaspoons
o Sesame seeds	1 tablespoon	1 1/4 tablespoons	1 ½ tablespoons
o Dried onions	1 1/3 tablespoons	1 2/3 tablespoons	2 tablespoons
o Baking powder	5/6 teaspoon	1 teaspoon	1¼ teaspoons
o Baking soda	1/3 teaspoon	7/16 teaspoon	½ teaspoon

Directions:

- Place all of the dry and liquid ingredients in the pan and follow the bread machine's directions.
- Pay close attention to the ingredient measurements. To do so, use a measuring cup, a measuring spoon, and kitchen scales.
- Select the Quick/Rapid baking program and the Medium crust type.
- Adjust the quantity of flour and liquid in the recipe if the dough is too dense or too wet.
- When the program is finished, remove the pan from the bread machine and set it aside for 5 minutes to cool.
- Remove the bread from the pan by shaking it. Use a spatula if needed.
- Allow to cool for a few minutes for around 10 minutes on a cooling rack.
- Serve and enjoy.

Note: *Quantities may require minor adjustments based on taste preference and desired consistency. As always, I recommend that you monitor the consistency of the dough during preparation, as you may need to make minor adjustments depending on your bread machine.*

8.1. Gluten-Free Simple Sandwich Bread

PREP. TIME: 10 MINUTES | COOK: 1 HOUR 10 MINUTES

SERVING:1 LB. 8-10 SLICES|1,5 LBS. 12-15 SLICES| 2 LBS. 16- 20 SLICES

PER SERVING: CALORIES 137 | TOTAL FAT 4G | PROTEIN 3G | CARBS 22G

Ingredient	1 Lb.	1.5 Lbs.	2 Lbs.
o Sorghum flour	1 cup	1 1/2 cups	2 cups
o Potato starch	2/3 cup	1 cup	1 1/3 cups
o Gluten-free oat flour	1/4 cup	1/3 cup	1/2 cup
o Xanthan gum	1 and 1/3 teaspoons	2 teaspoons	2 and 2/3 teaspoons
o Fine sea salt	Just under 1 teaspoon	1 and 1/4 teaspoons	1 and 2/3 teaspoons
o Gluten-free yeast	1 and 2/3 teaspoons	2 and 1/2 teaspoons	3 and 1/3 teaspoons
o Warm water	Just under 1 and 1/4 cups	1 and 1/4 cups	1 and 2/3 cups
o Extra virgin olive oil	2 tablespoons	3 tablespoons	4 tablespoons
o Honey	2/3 tablespoon	1 tablespoon	1 and 1/3 tablespoons
o Lemon juice	1/3 teaspoon	1/2 teaspoon	2/3 teaspoon
o Organic free-range eggs, beaten	1 egg	2 eggs	3 eggs

Directions:

- Start by combining all the dry ingredients except for the yeast. Once mixed, set them aside.
- In the bread machine pan, carefully pour in all the liquid components.
- Over the liquid, gently add your previously combined dry ingredients.
- Create a small well in the middle of the dry mixture. Pour the yeast into this well.
- Choose the "Gluten-Free" option on your bread machine. If your machine doesn't have this specific option, set the temperature to 350°F and the baking time to 1 hour and 10 minutes. Choose a medium crust color and press start.
- Once the baking cycle is complete, remove the bread and let it cool for approximately 15 minutes. After it has cooled down, slice and serve. Enjoy!
- The bread should sound hollow when tapped on the bottom.

8.2. Gluten-Free Brown Bread

PREP. TIME: 10 MINUTES | COOK: 3 HOURS

SERVING:1 LB. 12-14 SLICES|1,5 LBS. 18-22 SLICES| 2 LBS. 24- 28 SLICES

PER SERVING: CALORIES 201 | TOTAL FAT 6G | PROTEIN 5G | CARBS 35G

Ingredient	1 Lb.	1.5 Lbs.	2 Lbs.
o *Large eggs, lightly beaten*	2 eggs	3 eggs	4 eggs
o *Warm water*	1 and 3/4 cups	2 and 5/8 cups	3 and 1/2 cups
o *Canola oil*	3 tablespoons	4 and 1/2 tablespoons	6 tablespoons
o *Brown rice flour*	1 cup	1 and 1/2 cups	2 cups
o *Oat flour*	3/4 cup	1 and 1/8 cups	1 and 1/2 cups
o *Tapioca starch*	1/4 cup	3/8 cup	1/2 cup
o *Potato starch*	1 and 1/4 cups	1 and 7/8 cups	2 and 1/2 cups
o *Salt*	1 and 1/2 teaspoons	2 and 1/4 teaspoons	3 teaspoons
o *Brown sugar*	2 tablespoons	3 tablespoons	4 tablespoons
o *Gluten-free flaxseed meal*	2 tablespoons	3 tablespoons	4 tablespoons
o *Nonfat dry milk powder*	1/2 cup	3/4 cup	1 cup
o *Xanthan gum*	2 and 1/2 teaspoons	3 and 3/4 teaspoons	5 teaspoons
o *Psyllium, whole husks*	3 tablespoons	4 and 1/2 tablespoons	6 tablespoons
o *Gluten-free yeast*	2 and 1/2 teaspoons	3 and 3/4 teaspoons	5 teaspoons

Directions:

- In the bread machine pan, combine the eggs, water, and canola oil.
- In a large mixing bowl, mix all dry ingredients, excluding the yeast.
- Add the mixed dry ingredients over the liquid components in the bread machine.
- Form a small well in the middle of the dry mix. Place the yeast inside this well.
- Choose the "Gluten-Free" option. If your machine lacks this specific function, set it to 350°F and bake for 3 hours. Opt for a medium crust color and initiate the baking cycle.
- After baking concludes, overturn the bread to allow it to cool. Once adequately cooled, slice and serve.
- The bread should possess a nice brown crust when completely baked.

8.3. Gluten-Free Crusty Boule Bread

PREP. TIME: 15 MINUTES | COOK: 3 HOURS

SERVING:1 LB. 8 SLICES|1,5 LBS. 12 SLICES| 2 LBS. 16 SLICES

PER SERVING: CALORIES 480 | TOTAL FAT 3G | PROTEIN 2G | CARBS 49G

Ingredient	1 Lb.	1.5 Lbs.	2 Lbs.
o Gluten-free flour mix	2 and 1/6 cups	3 and 1/4 cups	4 and 1/3 cups
o Active dry yeast	2/3 tablespoon	1 tablespoon	1 and 1/3 tablespoons
o Kosher salt	1 teaspoon	1 and 1/2 teaspoons	2 teaspoons
o Guar gum	2/3 tablespoon	1 tablespoon	1 and 1/3 tablespoons
o Warm water	Just under 1 cup	1 and 1/3 cups	1 and 3/4 cups
o Large eggs, room temperature	1 and 1/3 eggs (consider 1 egg)	2 eggs	2 and 2/3 eggs (consider 3 eggs)
o Olive oil	1 and 1/2 tablespoons + 1 and 1/3 teaspoons	2 tablespoons + 2 teaspoons	3 tablespoons + 2 teaspoons
o Honey	2/3 tablespoon	1 tablespoon	1 and 1/3 tablespoons

Directions:

- In a large mixing bowl, combine all the dry ingredients without the yeast and set aside.
- In a separate mixing bowl, blend together the honey, water, eggs, & oil.
- Add the wet ingredients into the bread machine first.
- Carefully add the dry ingredients on top of the wet ingredients.
- Make a small well in the middle of the dry ingredients and add the yeast.
- Select the Gluten-Free setting, choose a medium crust. If your bread machine doesn't have a specific "Gluten-Free" option, use a baking cycle of 3 hours. Press the Start button.
- Once the baking cycle is finished, let the bread cool completely. You can either hollow out the center and fill with dip or soup to serve as a boule or simply slice and serve.

Note: *Quantities may require minor adjustments based on taste preference and desired consistency. As always, I recommend that you monitor the consistency of the dough during preparation, as you may need to make minor adjustments depending on your bread machine.*

PREP TIME: 15 MINUTES | COOK: 3 HOURS

SERVING:1 LB. 8 SLICES|1,5 LBS. 12 SLICES| 2 LBS. 16 SLICES

PER SERVING: CALORIES 271 | TOTAL FAT 4G | PROTEIN 5G | CARBS 29G

Ingredient	1 Lb.	1.5 Lbs.	2 Lbs.
o Sorghum flour	1½ cups	2 and 1/4 cups	3 cups
o Brown or white sweet rice flour	½ cup	3/4 cup	1 cup
o Tapioca starch	1 cup	1 and 1/2 cups	2 cups
o Xanthan gum	1 tsp.	1 and 1/2 tsp.	2 tsp.
o Guar gum	1 tsp.	1 and 1/2 tsp.	2 tsp.
o Salt	½ tsp.	3/4 tsp.	1 tsp.
o Sugar	3 tablespoons	4 and 1/2 tablespoons	6 tablespoons
o Instant yeast	2¼ tsp.	3 and 1/3 tsp.	4½ tsp.
o Oil	¼ cup	3/8 cup (or 6 tablespoons)	½ cup
o Eggs (lightly beaten at room temperature)	3 eggs	4 eggs (rounding up for convenience)	6 eggs
o Vinegar	1½ tsp.	2 and 1/4 tsp.	3 tsp.
o Milk (105 ºF to 115 ºF)	3/4 to 1 cup	1 and 1/8 to 1 and 1/2 cups	1 and 1/2 to 2 cups

Directions:

- Except for the yeast, put all of the dry ingredients in the mixing dish.
- Place the wet ingredients in the bread maker pan first, followed by the dry ingredients.
- In the middle of the dry ingredients, Make an indentation and add the yeast.
- Set the Gluten-Free bread cycle to light crust color and hit the Start button.
- Take the bread out of the pan and cool on a wire rack before serving.

Note: *Quantities may require minor adjustments based on taste preference and desired consistency. As always, I recommend that you monitor the consistency of the dough during preparation, as you may need to make minor adjustments depending on your bread machine.*

8.5. Gluten-Free Oat Bread

PREP TIME: 15 MINUTES | COOK: 3 HOURS

SERVING:1 LB. 8 SLICES|1,5 LBS. 12 SLICES| 2 LBS. 16 SLICES

PER SERVING: CALORIES 189 | TOTAL FAT 4G | PROTEIN 5G | CARBS 31G

Ingredient	1 Lb.	1.5 Lbs.	2 Lbs.
o *Warm water*	3/4 cup	1¼ cups	1 and 2/3 cups
o *Honey*	2 tablespoons	3 tablespoons	4 tablespoons
o *Eggs*	1 egg	2 eggs	3 eggs
o *Melted butter*	2 tablespoons	3 tablespoons	4 tablespoons
o *Gluten-free oats*	3/4 cup	1¼ cups	1 and 2/3 cups
o *Brown rice flour*	3/4 cup	1¼ cups	1 and 2/3 cups
o *Potato starch*	1/3 cup	½ cup	2/3 cup
o *Xanthan gum*	1 and 1/3 teaspoon	2 teaspoons	2 and 2/3 teaspoons
o *Sugar*	1 teaspoon	1½ teaspoon	2 teaspoons
o *Salt*	½ teaspoon	¾ teaspoon	1 teaspoon
o *Active dry yeast*	1 tablespoon	1½ tablespoons	2 tablespoons

Directions:

- Start by pouring the liquid ingredients (warm water, honey, eggs, and melted butter) into the bread machine pan.
- In a different bowl, add the dry ingredients excluding the yeast & mix (gluten-free oats, salt, brown rice flour, sugar, potato starch & xanthan gum).
- Gradually add this dry mixture over the liquid ingredients in the bread machine pan.
- Create a small indentation in the middle of the dry ingredients and add the active dry yeast.
- Choose the Gluten-Free cycle, select the light crust setting, and then press the Start button.
- After baking, let the bread cool for 20 minutes on a cooling rack before slicing and serving.

8.6. Gluten-Free Chia Bread

PREP TIME: 10 MINUTES | COOK TIME: 3 HOURS

SERVING:1 LB. 8 SLICES|1,5 LBS. 12 SLICES| 2 LBS. 16 SLICES

PER SERVING: CALORIES 375 | TOTAL FAT 18G | PROTEIN 12G | CARBS 42G

Ingredient	1 Lb.	1.5 Lbs.	2 Lbs.
o *Warm water*	2/3 cup	1 cup	1 and 1/3 cup
o *Large organic eggs, room temperature*	2 eggs	3 eggs	4 eggs
o *Olive oil*	2 and 2/3 tablespoons	1/4 cup	1/3 cup
o *Apple cider vinegar*	2 teaspoons	1 tablespoon	4 teaspoons
o *Gluten-free chia seeds (ground into flour)*	2/3 cup	1 cup	1 and 1/3 cup
o *Almond meal flour*	2/3 cup	1 cup	1 and 1/3 cup
o *Potato starch*	1/3 cup	1/2 cup	2/3 cup
o *Coconut flour*	2 and 2/3 tablespoons	1/4 cup	1/3 cup
o *Millet flour*	1/2 cup	3/4 cup	1 cup
o *Xanthan gum*	2 teaspoons	1 tablespoon	4 teaspoons
o *Salt*	1 teaspoon	1 1/2 teaspoons	2 teaspoons
o *Sugar*	1 and 1/3 tablespoon	2 tablespoons	2 and 2/3 tablespoons
o *Nonfat dry milk*	2 tablespoons	3 tablespoons	4 tablespoons
o *Instant yeast*	1 and 1/3 tablespoon	2 tablespoons	2 and 2/3 tablespoons

Directions:

- Start by adding the wet ingredients (warm water, eggs, olive oil, and apple cider vinegar) to the bread machine pan.
- Mix the dry ingredients (excluding the yeast) in a different bowl, then pour them over the wet mixture in the bread machine pan.
- Add the yeast to the dry ingredients after making a well in them. Set the bread machine to the Gluten-Free cycle, light crust setting, and press Start.
- Allow the bread to cool thoroughly before slicing. Enjoy.

8.7. Gluten-Free Paleo Bread

PREP. TIME: 10 MINUTES | COOK: 3 HOURS 15 MINUTES

SERVING:1 LB. 8 SLICES|1,5 LBS. 12 SLICES| 2 LBS. 16 SLICES

PER SERVING: CALORIES 190 | TOTAL FAT 10G | PROTEIN 5G | CARBS 21G

Ingredient	1 Lb.	1.5 Lbs.	2 Lbs.
o Chia seeds	2 tablespoons	3 tablespoons	4 tablespoons
o Flax meal (divided)	3/4 cup	1 cup + 3 tablespoons	1 1/4 cups
o Water	3/4 cup	1 1/8 cups	1 1/2 cups
o Coconut oil	2 tablespoons	3 tablespoons	1/4 cup
o Eggs, room temperature	2 eggs	2 eggs	3 eggs
o Almond milk	1/4 cup	6 tablespoons	1/2 cup
o Honey	1/2 tablespoon	3/4 tablespoon	1 tablespoon
o Almond flour	1 cup	1.5 cups	2 cups
o Tapioca flour	1 1/4 cups	1 1/4 cups + 3 tablespoons	1 1/4 cups
o Coconut flour	roughly 2.5 tablespoons	1/4 cup + 1/2 tablespoon	1/3 cup
o Salt	1/2 teaspoon	3/4 teaspoon	1 teaspoon
o Cream of tartar	1 teaspoon	1.5 teaspoons	2 teaspoons
o Baking soda	1/2 teaspoon	3/4 teaspoon	1 teaspoon
o Active dry yeast	1 teaspoon	1.5 teaspoons	2 teaspoons

Directions:

- In a bowl, mix the chia seeds and 1 tbsp of flax meal. Add water, stir, and set aside to allow it to achieve a gel-like consistency. Microwave the coconut oil in the microwave until melted, then let it cool for a few minutes.
- Mix the honey, eggs & almond milk together. Incorporate the chia seed and flax meal mixture. Add this blend into the bread machine pan.
- In a separate mixing bowl, combine almond flour, coconut flour, tapioca flour, salt, and the rest of the flax meal. In another small bowl, mix the baking soda and cream of tartar together.
- Layer all dry ingredients over the wet mixture inside the bread machine. Make a small well in the middle and add the yeast. Set your machine to the Gluten-Free cycle, opt for either light/medium crust, and press Start.
- After baking, ensure the bread cools down completely before slicing to serve. Enjoy!

9.1. Almond Flour Bread

PREP. TIME: 10 MINUTES | COOK TIME: 1 HOUR

SERVING:1 LB. 12 SLICES|1,5 LBS. 18 SLICES| 2 LBS. 24 SLICES

PER SERVING: CALORIES 110 | TOTAL FAT 10G | PROTEIN 4G | CARBS 17G

Ingredient	1 Lb.	1.5 Lbs.	2 Lbs.
o Egg yolks	2	3	4
o Egg whites	4	6	8
o Almond flour	2 cups	3 cups	4 cups
o Butter, melted	1/4 cup	3/8 cup	1/2 cup
o Psyllium husk powder	2 tablespoons	3 tablespoons	4 tablespoons
o Baking powder	1 1/2 tablespoons	2 1/4 tablespoons	3 tablespoons
o Xanthan gum	1/2 teaspoon	3/4 teaspoon	1 teaspoon
o Salt	To taste	To taste	To taste
o Warm water	1/2 cup + 2 tablespoons	3/4 cup + 3 tablespoons	1 cup + 4 tablespoons
o Yeast	2 1/4 teaspoons	3 1/3 teaspoons	4 1/2 teaspoons

Directions:

- Begin with the yeast, combine it with the warm water in a separate bowl and let it sit for 5-10 minutes until it becomes frothy.
- In another bowl, mix together all the dry ingredients, excluding the yeast.
- In the bread machine pan, combine all wet ingredients.
- Gradually add the mixed dry ingredients to the machine. Pour in the activated yeast mixture.
- Set the bread machine to basic bread mode and choose the desired crust setting.
- Once done, remove the bread machine pan from the bread machine.
- Let the bread to cool slightly before transferring to a cooling rack.
- Store: The bread can be kept on the counter for up to 4 days or can be kept in the freezer for up to 3 months.

9.2. Coconut Flour Bread

PREP TIME: 10 MINUTES | COOK TIME: 1 HOUR

SERVING:1 LB. 8-10 SLICES|1,5 LBS. 12-15 SLICES| 2 LBS. 16-20 SLICES

PER SERVING: CALORIES 174 | TOTAL FAT 15G | PROTEIN 7G | CARBS 15G

Ingredient	1 Lb.	1.5 Lbs.	2 Lbs.
o Eggs	6	9	12
o Coconut flour	1/2 cup	3/4 cup	1 cup
o Psyllium husk	2 tablespoons	3 tablespoons	4 tablespoons
o Olive oil	1/4 cup	3/8 cup	1/2 cup
o Salt	1 1/2 teaspoons	2 1/4 teaspoons	3 teaspoons
o Xanthan gum	1 tablespoon	1 1/2 tablespoons	2 tablespoons
o Baking powder	1 tablespoon	1 1/2 tablespoons	2 tablespoons
o Yeast	2 1/4 teaspoons	3 1/3 teaspoons	4 1/2 teaspoons

Directions:

- Begin with the yeast, combine it with warm water in a separate bowl (not listed in ingredients, but typically used with yeast) and let it sit for 5-10 minutes until it becomes frothy.
- In another bowl, mix together all the dry ingredients, excluding the yeast.
- In the bread machine pan, combine the eggs and olive oil.
- Gradually add the mixed dry ingredients in the bread pan of the machine. Pour in the activated yeast mixture.
- Set the bread machine to basic bread mode and choose the desired crust setting.
- Once done, remove the bread machine pan from the bread machine.
- Let the bread cool slightly before transferring to a cooling rack.
- Store: The bread can be kept on the counter for up to 4 days or can be in the freezer for up to 3 months.

PREP.: 10 MINUTES | COOK: 2 TO 3 HOURS

SERVING:1 LB. 8-10 SLICES|1,5 LBS. 12-15 SLICES| 2 LBS. 16-20 SLICES

PER SERVING: CALORIES 198 | TOTAL FAT 5G | PROTEIN 5G | CARBS 34G

Ingredient	1 Lb.	1.5 Lbs.	2 Lbs.
o Water, at room 80°F	2/3 cup	1 cup	1 1/3 cups
o Whole egg, at room temp	1	1.5*	2
o Butter, melted and cooled	2 2/3 tablespoons	4 tablespoons	5 1/3 tablespoons
o Honey	2 2/3 tablespoons	4 tablespoons	5 1/3 tablespoons
o Salt	1/3 teaspoon	1/2 teaspoon	2/3 teaspoon
o Anise seed	2/3 teaspoon	1 teaspoon	1 1/3 teaspoons
o Lemon zest	2/3 teaspoon	1 teaspoon	1 1/3 teaspoons
o Almond flour	2 cups	3 cups	4 cups
o Instant yeast	1 1/3 teaspoons	2 teaspoons	2 2/3 teaspoons

* For recipes that call for an odd number of eggs (like 1.5), you could whisk 2 eggs and use about 75% of the mixture.

Directions:

- Follow the manufacturer's instructions when adding the indicated ingredients to your bread machine.
- Set the bread machine to the Basic/White Bread program and the crust type to Light. Start the program.
- Wait till the last bake cycle is finished.
- When the loaf is finished, take the bucket out of the bread machine and set it aside for five minutes.
- Shake the bucket gently to release the loaf, then place it on a cooling rack to cool before slicing.
- Serve and enjoy!

9.4. Cardamom Bread

Prep. time: 10 minutes | Cook time: 1 hour 20 minutes

Serving:1 lb. 8-10 slices|1,5 lbs. 12-15 slices| 2 lbs. 16-20 slices

Per Serving: Calories 149 | Total Fat 2g | Protein 5g | Carbs 29g

Ingredient	1 Lb.	1.5 Lbs.	2 Lbs.
○ Milk, 80°F to 90°F	½ cup	¾ cup	1 cup
○ Egg at room temperature	1	1.5*	2
○ Butter, melted and cooled	1 teaspoon	1.5 teaspoons	2 teaspoons
○ Honey	4 teaspoons	6 teaspoons	8 teaspoons
○ Salt	2/3 teaspoon	1 teaspoon	1 1/3 teaspoons
○ Cardamom, ground	2/3 teaspoon	1 teaspoon	1 1/3 teaspoons
○ Coconut flour	2 cups	3 cups	4 cups
○ Bread machine or instant yeast	3/4 teaspoon	1 1/8 teaspoons	1 1/2 teaspoons

*For recipes that call for an odd number of eggs (like 1.5), you could whisk 2 eggs and use about 75% of the mixture.

Directions:

- Put all the ingredients in your bread maker as per the manufacturer's instructions.
- Choose Basic/White bread, choose the desired crust, and click the Start button.
- Remove the bucket from the machine when the bread is finished.
- Allow 5 minutes for the bread to cool.
- Shake the bucket gently to extract the loaf, then place it on a cooling rack to cool.
- Serve and enjoy.

9.5. Honey-Spice Egg Bread

PREP. TIME: 10 MINUTES | COOK: 3 HOURS 15 MINUTES

SERVING: 1 LB. 8-10 SLICES | 1,5 LBS. 12-15 SLICES | 2 LBS. 16-20 SLICES

PER SERVING: CALORIES 111 | TOTAL FAT 4G | PROTEIN 3G | CARBS 9G

Ingredient	1 Lb.	1.5 Lbs.	2 Lbs.
o *Fresh eggs*	1⅓	2	2⅔
o *Warm water*	⅔ cup	1 cup	1⅓ cup
o *Unsalted butter*	1 tablespoon	1 ½ tablespoons	2 tablespoons
o *Honey*	1⅓ tablespoons	2 tablespoons	2⅔ tablespoons
o *Salt*	⅔ teaspoon	1 teaspoon	1⅓ teaspoons
o *Powdered milk*	2 tablespoons	3 tablespoons	4 tablespoons
o *Almond flour*	2 cups	3 cups	4 cups
o *Active dry yeast*	1⅓ teaspoons	2 teaspoons	2⅔ teaspoons
o *Cinnamon*	⅔ teaspoon	1 teaspoon	1⅓ teaspoons
o *Cardamom*	⅔ teaspoon	1 teaspoon	1⅓ teaspoons
o *Ginger*	⅔ teaspoon	1 teaspoon	1⅓ teaspoons
Nutmeg	⅔ teaspoon	1 teaspoon	1⅓ teaspoons

Directions:

- Put all the ingredients into the bread maker in the sequence recommended by the manufacturer.
- Choose white bread with a light crust. Start the program.
- Once finished baking, remove from the baking machine pan and serve warm with butter or honey.

Note: Quantities may require minor adjustments based on taste preference and desired consistency. As always, I recommend that you monitor the consistency of the dough during preparation, as you may need to make minor adjustments depending on your bread machine.

Due to the rich combination of spices in this bread, you may wish to start with slightly less of each spice initially, tasting the dough and adjusting according to personal preference. Remember, it's always easier to add more spices than to correct an overly spiced dough.

9.6. Flaxseed Bread

PREP TIME: 10 MINUTES | COOK TIME: 3 HOURS

SERVING: 1 LB. 8-10 SLICES | 1,5 LBS. 12-15 SLICES | 2 LBS. 16-20 SLICES

PER SERVING: CALORIES 122 | TOTAL FAT 5G | PROTEIN 4G | CARBS 8G

Ingredient		1 Lb.	1.5 Lbs.	2 Lbs.
o	Ground flaxseeds	1 ½ cups	2¼ cups	3 cups
o	Almond flour	¼ cup	⅜ cup	½ cup
o	Instant bread yeast	2 tsps.	3 tsps.	4 tsps.
o	Salt	½ tsp.	¾ tsp.	1 tsp.
o	Large eggs	4	6	8
o	Melted coconut oil	¼ cup	⅜ cup	½ cup
o	Water	½ cup	¾ cup	1 cup

Directions:

- Combine the ground flaxseeds, almond flour, instant bread yeast, and salt.
- Separately, beat the eggs, then add the melted coconut oil and water. Combine thoroughly.
- Add the wet ingredients to the dry ingredients in the bread machine pan.
- On the bread machine, select the "Quick Bread" or "Cake" mode. If you have a 1.5-pound loaf setting with a medium crust, adjust the parameters accordingly.
- Start the machine and let it mix and bake the bread based on your selected settings.
- Once the baking cycle is complete, carefully take the bread out of the pan and place on a wire rack to cool before slicing.
- Serve and enjoy.

Note: *Quantities may require minor adjustments based on taste preference and desired consistency. As always, I recommend that you monitor the consistency of the dough during preparation, as you may need to make minor adjustments depending on your bread machine.*

Before starting the baking cycle, consider brushing the bread with a little melted coconut oil or beaten egg to get a crispy crust.

PREP TIME: 10 MINUTES | COOK TIME: 3 HOURS

SERVING:1 LB. 8-10 SLICES|1,5 LBS. 12-15 SLICES| 2 LBS. 16-20 SLICES

PER SERVING: CALORIES 102 | TOTAL FAT 3G | PROTEIN 4G | CARBS 9G

Ingredient		1 Lb.	1.5 Lbs.	2 Lbs.
o	Almond flour	1 ½ cups	2¼ cups	3 cups
o	Ground psyllium husk powder	½ cup	¾ cup	1 cup
o	Baking powder	2 tsps.	3 tsps.	4 tsps.
o	Salt	1 tsp.	1½ tsps.	2 tsps.
o	Large eggs	4	6	8
o	Melted coconut oil	¼ cup	⅜ cup	½ cup
o	Warm water (100°F/110°F)	1 cup	1½ cups	2 cups

Directions:

• Combine almond flour, ground psyllium husk powder, baking powder, and salt.

• Ensure the warm water is about 100°F to 110°F.

• In a different bowl, whisk the eggs, then incorporate the melted coconut oil and warm water. Mix well.

• Add the wet ingredients to the dry ingredients in the bread machine pan.

• Choose the "Quick Bread" or "Cake" mode on your bread machine. Adjust parameters if you use a 1.5-pound loaf setting with a medium crust.

• Start your machine and allow it to mix and bake the bread based on the chosen settings.

• After the baking cycle ends, take the bread out of the pan carefully and cool on a wire rack before slicing.

Note: *Quantities may require minor adjustments based on taste preference and desired consistency. As always, I recommend that you monitor the consistency of the dough during preparation, as you may need to make minor adjustments depending on your bread machine.*

10.1. Sourdough Dinner Rolls

PREP. TIME: 10 MINUTES | COOK TIME: 1 HOUR 20 MINUTES

SERVING:1 LB. 16 ROLLS|1,5 LBS. 24 ROLLS| 2 LBS. 36 ROLLS

PER SERVING: CALORIES 128 | TOTAL FAT 3G | PROTEIN 4G | CARBS 29G

Ingredient	1 Lb.	1.5 Lbs.	2 Lbs.
o *Sourdough starter*	2/3 cup	1 cup	1 1/3 cups
o *Warm water (100°F to 110°F.)*	1 cup	1½ cups	2 cups
o *Yeast*	2/3 tablespoon	1 tablespoon	1 1/3 tablespoons
o *Salt*	2/3 tablespoon	1 tablespoon	1 1/3 tablespoons
o *Sugar*	1 1/3 tablespoons	2 tablespoons	2 2/3 tablespoons
o *Olive oil*	1 1/3 tablespoons	2 tablespoons	2 2/3 tablespoons
o *All-purpose flour*	2 2/3 cups	4 cups	5 1/3 cups
o *Melted butter*	1 1/3 tablespoons	2 tablespoons	2 2/3 tablespoons

Directions:

- In the bread machine pan, combine all of the liquid components, including the sourdough starter, warm water, and olive oil.
- Add the yeast to the liquid components, being careful not to let it come into touch with the salt.
- Over the liquid mixture, sprinkle the sugar.
- On top of the liquids and sugar, add the bread flour.
- Finally, sprinkle the flour with the salt.
- Start the cycle on your bread machine with the dough setting. The machine will combine the ingredients, knead the dough, and allow it to rise.
- When the dough cycle has finished, take it out of the bread machine and place it on a floured surface.
- Form the dough into rolls by dividing it into 2-3 inch sections.
- Grease a 9x13-inch baking pan and arrange the rolls inside.
- Cover the pan using a clean cloth and set aside for an hour to allow the rolls to rise.
- Preheat the oven at 350°F.
- Bake for 15 minutes or until the rolls are golden brown.
- After baking the rolls, brush them with the melted butter.
- Return the rolls to the oven and bake for 5-10 minutes more or until well-browned and cooked through.
- Allow the rolls to cool slightly before serving.

10.2. Laminated Croissants

PREP. TIME: 10 MINUTES | COOK: 1 HOUR 30 MINUTES

CROISSANT:1 LB. 7 |1,5 LBS. 10| 2 LBS.14

PER SERVING: CALORIES 315 | TOTAL FAT 4G | PROTEIN 5G | CARBS 27G

Ingredient	1 Lb.	1.5 Lbs.	2 Lbs.
o Bread flour	1 ⅓ cups	2 cups	2 ⅔ cups
o Instant yeast	1 teaspoon	1 ½ teaspoons	2 teaspoons
o Sugar	⅙ cup	¼ cup	⅓ cup
o Salt	⅔ teaspoon	1 teaspoon	1 ⅓ teaspoons
o Milk	⅓ cup	½ cup	⅔ cup
o Water	⅓ cup	½ cup	⅔ cup
o Unsalted butter, cold	⅔ cup	1 cup	1 ⅓ cups

Directions:

- Combine sugar, salt, milk, water, bread flour, and instant yeast in the following sequence inside the bread machine pan. Select the Dough cycle and push the Start button.
- As the dough cycle completes, take it to a floured board and shape it into a rectangle.
- Between two sheets of parchment paper, flatten the cold, unsalted butter into a rectangle.
- Put the butter in the middle of the dough and fold the sides over to encase it.
- Roll out the dough-butter mixture and fold it into thirds (as if it were a letter). Rep this process three times.
- Refrigerate the dough for 1 hour in between folds.
- Shape the dough into croissants, crescents, or other desired forms after the final round of folds.
- Place the formed dough on a parchment-lined baking sheet.
- Allow to rise for 1-2 hours, covered loosely using a clean tea towel.
- Let the oven preheat to 375°F.
- Bake the croissants for 15-20 minutes or until golden brown and flaky.
- Allow the croissants to cool for a few minutes before serving.

Note: *Before baking, consider brushing the croissants with a mixture of 1 beaten egg and a tablespoon of milk or water. This gives them a glossy, golden finish when baked.*

Baking Tip: *It's essential to watch the croissants closely towards the end of the baking time to avoid over-browning. The ideal croissant is golden and flaky on the outside with a soft, airy interior.*

10.3. Polish Baguette

PREPARATION TIME: 10 MINUTES | COOKING TIME: 2 HOURS

LOAF :1 LB. 4 -6|1,5 LBS. 6-8| 2 LBS. 8-10

PER SERVING: CALORIES 278 | TOTAL FAT 4G | PROTEIN 11G | CARBS 29G

Ingredient	1 Lb.	1.5 Lbs.	2 Lbs.
for Polish:			
o Bread flour	⅔ cup	1 cup	1 ⅓ cups
o Water	⅓ cup	½ cup	⅔ cup
o Instant yeast	A smaller pinch	Pinch	A slightly bigger pinch
for Final Dough:			
o All the polish	Proportional based on above	All the polish	Proportional based on above
o Bread flour	1 ⅓ cups	2 cups	2 ⅔ cups
o Salt	⅓ teaspoon	½ teaspoon	⅔ teaspoon
o Instant yeast	⅔ teaspoon	1 teaspoon	1 ⅓ teaspoons
o Water	⅔ cup	1 cup	1 ⅓ cups

Directions:

- To make the polish, combine bread flour, water, and instant yeast. Allow it to ferment for 12-16 hours at room temperature.
- Combine the polish, water, more bread flour, salt, and instant yeast in the bread machine pan. Select the Dough cycle and push the Start button.
- As the dough cycle completes, put it on a floured board and form it as desired (loaf, rolls, etc.).
- Place the formed dough in oiled baking pans or on a parchment-lined baking sheet.
- Allow to rise for 1-2 hours, covered loosely using a clean tea towel.
- Preheat the oven at 450°F (230°C)
- Bake for around 20-25 minutes (for rolls) or 30-35 minutes (for a loaf), or until golden brown and the bottom sounds hollow when tapped.
- Let the bread cool completely before slicing.

Baking for Crisp Crust: For a more traditional, crisp crust on your baguette, consider placing a baking dish with boiling water on the lowest rack of the oven during the baking process or spritzing the inside of the oven with water. This will create steam which aids in achieving that signature crunchy crust.

Baguette Characteristics: A well-baked baguette should have a golden, crispy crust with a soft, airy interior. Adjust baking time slightly as necessary to achieve this finish.

Polish Benefits: Using a polish starter not only adds to the flavor but also improves the overall texture and shelf-life of the baguette. Ensure you allow it adequate fermentation time.

PREP. TIME: 15 MINUTES | COOK: 2 HOURS

LOAF :1 LB. 4 -6|1,5 LBS. 6-8| 2 LBS. 8-10

PER SERVING: CALORIES 199 | TOTAL FAT 6G | PROTEIN 7G | CARBS 31G

Ingredient	1 Lb.	1.5 Lbs.	2 Lbs.
For Biga:			
o Bread flour	¾ cup	1 ¼ cups	1 ½ cups
o Instant yeast	¼ teaspoon	⅜ teaspoon	½ teaspoon
o Water, room temperature	⅜ cup	⅝ cup	¾ cup
Final Dough:			
o All the biga	Proportional based on above	Proportional based on above	All the biga
o Bread flour	1 ¼ cups	2 cups	2 ½ cups
o Salt	½ teaspoon	¾ teaspoon	1 teaspoon
o Instant yeast	½ teaspoon	¾ teaspoon	1 teaspoon
o Water	½ cup	¾ cup	1 cup

Directions:

- Mix bread flour, instant yeast, and water to make the biga. Allow it to ferment for 12-24 hours at room temperature.
- Combine the biga, water, more bread flour, salt, and instant yeast in the bread machine pan. Select the Dough cycle and push the Start button.
- When the dough cycle is through, place it on a floured board and form it as desired (loaf, rolls, etc.).
- Place the formed dough in oiled baking pans or on a parchment-lined baking sheet.
- Allow to rise for 1-2 hours, covered loosely with a clean tea towel.
- Preheat the oven at 450°F (230°C).
- Bake for around 20-25 minutes (for rolls) or 30-35 minutes (for a loaf), or until golden brown and the bottom sounds hollow when tapped.
- Let it cool completely before slicing.

Note: Quantities may require minor adjustments based on taste preference and desired consistency. As always, I recommend that you monitor the consistency of the dough during preparation, as you may need to make minor adjustments depending on your bread machine.

10.5. Tangthong Milk Bread

PREP. TIME: 15 MINUTES | COOK TIME: 2 HOURS

LOAF :1 LB. 4 -5|1,5 LBS. 5-6| 2 LBS. 6-8

PER SERVING: CALORIES 217 | TOTAL FAT 7G | PROTEIN 3G | CARBS 32G

Ingredient	1 Lb.	1.5 Lbs.	2 Lbs.
for Tangthong:			
o Bread flour	1 ½ tablespoons	2 ¼ tablespoons	3 tablespoons
o Water	¼ cup	⅜ cup	½ cup
for Final Dough:			
o All the Tangthong	Proportional based on above	Proportional based on above	All the Tangthong
o Bread flour	1 ¾ cups	2 ⅝ cups	3 ½ cups
o Sugar	2 tablespoons	3 tablespoons	¼ cup
o Salt	½ teaspoon	¾ teaspoon	1 teaspoon
o Instant yeast	¾ teaspoon	1 ⅛ teaspoons	1 ½ teaspoons
o Milk	¼ cup	⅜ cup	½ cup
o Unsalted butter, softened	2 tablespoons	3 tablespoons	¼ cup

Directions:

- In a small pan, mix bread flour and water for the Tangthong. Cook over a low flame, stirring continuously, until it turns into a thick gel-like consistency. This usually takes about 5 minutes. Let it cool to room temperature.
- In the bread machine pan, combine the cooled Tangthong, milk, softened butter, bread flour, sugar, salt, and instant yeast. Opt for the Dough cycle and press the Start button.
- Once the dough cycle finishes, transfer the dough to a floured board and shape as preferred (loaf, rolls, etc.).
- Position the shaped dough in greased baking pans or on a parchment paper-lined baking tray.
- Let it rise for 1-2 hours, loosely covered with a clean tea towel.
- Lower the oven temperature for this bread to 375°F (190°C) and preheat. Tangzhong bread bakes best at this slightly lower temperature.
- Bake for about 20-25 minutes (if making rolls) or 30-35 minutes (for a loaf). The bread should turn golden brown, and the bottom should produce a hollow sound when tapped.
- Let the bread cool off entirely before cutting.

Note: Quantities may require minor adjustments based on taste preference and desired consistency. As always, I recommend that you monitor the consistency of the dough during preparation, as you may need to make minor adjustments depending on your bread machine.

11.1. Swedish Cardamom Bread

PREP. TIME: 15 MINUTES | COOK TIME: 2 HOURS

PIECES :1 LB. 3-4|1,5 LBS. 5-6| 2 LBS. 7-8

PER SERVING: CALORIES 135 | TOTAL FAT 7G | PROTEIN 3G | CARBS 22G

Ingredient	1 Lb.	1.5 Lbs.	2 Lbs.
o *Sugar*	¼ cup	⅜ cup	½ cup
o *Warm Milk*	¾ cup	1⅛ cups	1½ cups
o *Cardamom*	¾ tsp.	1⅛ tsps.	1½ tsps.
o *Salt*	½ tsp.	¾ tsp.	1 tsp.
o *Softened Butter*	¼ cup	⅜ cup	½ cup
o *Egg*	1	1½ (or 1 large and 1 small)	2
o *Bread Machine Yeast*	2¼ tsps.	3⅜ tsps.	4½ tsps.
o *All-purpose Flour*	3 cups	4½ cups	6 cups
o *Milk for Brushing*	5 tbsps.	7½ tbsps.	10 tbsps.
o *Sugar for Sprinkling*	2 tbsps.	3 tbsps.	4 tbsps.

Directions:

- In the pan of your bread machine, combine everything (except the milk for brushing and the sugar for dusting).
- Choose the dough cycle. Press the start button. As the cycle completes, you will have an elastic and smooth dough. It should be double the size.
- Place on a lightly floured surface.
- Now separate into three balls. Leave for 10 minutes.
- Roll all of the balls into 14-inch-long ropes.
- Braid the shapes together. Pinch the ends together tightly and place on a baking sheet. You can alternatively separate your dough into two balls. Smooth them out and place them on your bread pan.
- Brush milk through the braid. Lightly dust with sugar.
- Bake for 25 minutes at 375°F (190°C), ensuring to cover with foil for the last 10 minutes to prevent over-browning.

Note: Remember to keep an eye on the baking time when you change the loaf size, as larger loaves might need a bit more time in the oven. Always check for doneness by tapping on its base – if it sounds hollow, it's ready. Using a thermometer to check the internal temperature (around 190°F or 87°C) is also a good idea.

11.2. Winnipeg Rye Bread

PREP. TIME: 15 MIN. | COOK: 2 HOURS 40 MIN.

SLICES:1 LB. 4-5|1,5 LBS. 6-7| 2 LBS. 8-10

PER SERVING: CALORIES 145 | TOTAL FAT 3G | PROTEIN 2G | CARBS 26G

Ingredient	1 lb.	1.5 lbs.	2 lbs.
o Water	2 tablespoons	3 tablespoons	¼ cup
o Cracked Rye Berries	2 tablespoons	3 tablespoons	¼ cup
o Salt	1/2 teaspoon	¾ teaspoon	1 teaspoon
o Milk	1/3 cup	½ cup	3/4 cup
o Egg	1 egg	1 egg	1 egg
o Brown Sugar	2 tablespoons	3 tablespoons	1/4 cup
o Bread Flour	2 ¼ cups	3 ¼ cups	4 ¼ cups
o Butter	1.5 tablespoons	2 tablespoons	3 tablespoons
o Active Dry Yeast	1 teaspoon	1 ½ teaspoon	1 ¾ teaspoons
o Gluten	2 teaspoons	3 teaspoons	4 teaspoons
o Milk (for brushing)	½ tablespoon	¾ tablespoon	1 tablespoon

Directions:

- Soak the rye berries in the designated water. The majority should be absorbed.
- Incorporate all ingredients into the bread machine, followed by the soaked rye berries.
- Choose the Dough cycle and initiate.
- Once the cycle concludes, extract the dough.
- Deflate the dough and rest for 10 minutes.
- Separate the dough into two and shape into loaves.
- Place on a baking sheet, allowing them to rise for about 30 minutes until doubled.
- Let the oven preheat to 350°F (175°C).
- Brush the loaf tops with milk.
- Bake for approximately 35 to 40 minutes.
- Let it cool, then slice, serve, and enjoy.

Note: *Quantities may require minor adjustments based on taste preference and desired consistency. As always, I recommend that you monitor the consistency of the dough during preparation, as you may need to make minor adjustments depending on your bread machine.*

PREP. TIME: 20 MINUTES | COOK TIME: 2 HOURS

SLICES:1 LB. 4-5|1,5 LBS. 6-7| 2 LBS. 8-10

PER SERVING: CALORIES 213 | TOTAL FAT 4G | PROTEIN 5G | CARBS 32G

Ingredient	1 lb.	1.5 lbs.	2 lbs.
For the dough:			
o Fat-free Milk	¾ cup	1⅛ cup	1½ cup
o Fruity Olive Oil	¼ cup	⅜ cup	½ cup
o Large Egg	1 egg	1 egg + 1 yolk	2 eggs
o Bread Flour	3 cups	4½ cups	6 cups
o Honey (for dough)	¼ cup	⅜ cup	½ cup
o Grated Zest of Orange or Lemon	Zest of 1	Zest of 1½	Zest of 2
o Gluten	1 tablespoon	1½ tablespoon	2 tablespoons
o Salt	1½ teaspoons	2¼ teaspoons	3 teaspoons
o Apple Pie Spice	1 teaspoon	1½ teaspoon	2 teaspoons
o Bread Machine Yeast	1 tablespoon	1½ tablespoon	2 tablespoons
For the glaze:			
o Corn Syrup	2 tablespoons	3 tablespoons	¼ cup
o Honey	2 tablespoons	3 tablespoons	¼ cup
o Orange Juice	2 tablespoons	3 tablespoons	¼ cup
o White or Black Sesame Seeds (Nigella)	2 tablespoons	3 tablespoons	¼ cup

Directions:

- Place all the dough ingredients in the bread machine pan in the manufacturer recommended. Choose the Dough cycle and push the Start button. Please keep in mind that this recipe cannot be used with the Delay Timer feature.
- Using parchment paper, line a baking sheet. When the Dough cycle is finished, switch off and disconnect the machine. Put the dough on a work surface that is lightly floured. If you're adding extra ingredients, make the dough into a rectangle, add the extras on top, fold the dough over, and slowly knead to distribute them evenly. Place the dough in a tight circular form on the prepared baking pan. Cover loosely with greased plastic wrap and set aside for 1 hour to double in size.
- Let the oven preheat to 350°F (175°C) and place the rack in the bottom third position.
- Bake the bread for around 40-45 minutes, or until golden brown and the bottom should sound hollow when you tap with a finger.
- Remove the bread from the pan and cool for a few minutes on a wire rack before continuing with the glaze.
- In a small saucepan, combine the honey, corn syrup, and orange juice for the glaze. Bring the mixture to a boil and continue to boil for 60 seconds. Brush the top of the warm loaf with the glaze and sprinkle with sesame seeds.
- Before slicing and serving, allow the bread to cool completely.

11.4. Golden Pan dolce

PREP TIME: 20 MINUTES | COOK TIME: 2 HOURS

SLICES:1 LB. 4-5|1,5 LBS. 6-8| 2 LBS. 10-12

PER SERVING: CALORIES 264 | TOTAL FAT 7G | PROTEIN 6G | CARBS 41G

Ingredient	1 lb.	1,5 lbs.	2 lbs.
o Golden raisins	⅜ cup	⅝ cup	¾ cup
o Marsala wine (for raisins)	1½ tablespoon	2¼ tablespoon	3 tablespoons
o Milk	⅓ cup	½ cup	⅔ cup
o Water	⅓ cup	½ cup	⅔ cup
o Marsala wine	1½ tablespoon	2¼ tablespoon	3 tablespoons
o Olive oil	⅙ cup	¼ cup	⅓ cup
o Orange-flower water	¾ tablespoon	1 tablespoon + ¼ teaspoon	1½ tablespoon
o Vanilla extract	¾ teaspoon	1 teaspoon + ¼ teaspoon	1½ teaspoon
o Bread flour	2 cups	3 cups	4 cups
o Sugar	⅙ cup	¼ cup	⅓ cup
o Chopped pine nuts	2 tablespoons	3 tablespoons	¼ cup
o Gluten	2 teaspoons (roughly)	1 tablespoon	1 tablespoon + 2 teaspoon
o Salt	¾ teaspoon	1 teaspoon + ⅛ teaspoon	1½ teaspoon
o Aniseed, crushed	⅜ teaspoon	½ teaspoon + ⅛ teaspoon	¾ teaspoon
o Bread machine yeast	1⅓ teaspoon	2 teaspoons	2¾ teaspoon
o Butter (for topping)	¾ tablespoon	1 tablespoon + ¼ teaspoon	1½ tablespoon
o Sugar (for sprinkling)	1½ teaspoon	2½ teaspoon	1 tablespoon

Directions:

- Inside a small bowl, combine the golden raisins and Marsala wine.
- Allow them to macerate for 30 minutes at room temperature.
- Except for the raisins and the tablespoon of flour, combine all of the ingredients in the bread machine pan as per the manufacturer's directions. Select the Dough cycle and push the Start button. The finished dough ball will have a slightly soft texture.
- Using parchment paper, line a baking sheet. When the Dough cycle is finished, switch off and disconnect the machine. Shape the dough into a large rectangle on a lightly floured work surface. Lift the raisins from their liquor with a slotted spoon, then toss them with a tablespoon of flour. Keep the liquid aside.
- Fold the dough over and sprinkle with the macerated raisins. Gently mix the dough to properly distribute the raisins. Make two equal amounts of dough and shape each into a circular loaf. Place the loaves on the baking sheet that has been prepared. Cover loosely using a clean tea towel and put aside for 75 minutes to double in size.
- Preheat the oven at 350°F (175°C) with the center rack set about 20 minutes before baking.
- Cut an X on top of each loaf with a lamé or a very sharp knife. Remove one triangular piece of dough from the top of each loaf, forming an open "ear." Insert a bit of butter into the base of each ear, then fold back a small amount of each point over the butter. Trickle the set aside raisin-soaking liquid over the tops of the loaves and sprinkle with sugar.
- Let the loaves bake for around 35 to 40 minutes, or until golden brown and a finger tap on the bottom sounds hollow. Take the loaves out of the pan & place them on a rack to cool. Before slicing and serving, allow the loaves to cool completely.

Note: Quantities may require minor adjustments based on taste preference and desired consistency. As always, I recommend that you monitor the consistency of the dough during preparation, as you may need to make minor adjustments depending on your bread machine.

11.5. Marzipan Kringle

Prep. time: 20 minutes | Cook: 1 hour 50 minutes

Loaf:1 lb. 4|1,5 lbs. 6| 2 lbs. 8

Per Serving: Calories 198 | Total Fat 9g | Protein 5g | Carbs 35g

Ingredient	1 Lb.	1.5 Lbs.	2 Lbs.
For the dough:			
o Salt	¾ teaspoon	1⅛ teaspoon	1½ teaspoon
o Large egg yolks	1½	2¼	3
o Unsalted butter, cubed	3 tablespoons	4½ tablespoon	6 tablespoons
o Unbleached all-purpose flour	1¾ cup	2⅝ cup	3½ cups
o Sugar	2 tablespoons	3 tablespoons	¼ cup
o Light cream or whole milk	5/8 cup	15/16 cup	1 ¼ cups
o Bread machine yeast	1⅓ teaspoon	2 teaspoons	2¾ teaspoon
For the marzipan filling:			
o Almond paste	⅝ cup	15/16 cup	1 ¼ cups
o Sugar	¼ cup	⅜ cup	½ cup
o Egg white, beaten	½ egg white	¾ egg white	1 egg white
o Almond extract	½ teaspoon	¾ teaspoon	1 teaspoon
o Ground cinnamon	½ teaspoon	¾ teaspoon	1 teaspoon
o Chopped almonds	⅜ cup	9/16 cup	¾ cup
For the glaze and topping:			
o Raw sugar	1½ tablespoon	2¼ tablespoon	3 tablespoons
o Egg white, beaten with water	½	¾	1
o Sliced almonds	¼ cup	⅜ cup	½ cup

Directions:

- Fill the bread machine pan halfway with dough ingredients as per the manufacturer's directions. Choose the Dough cycle and push the Start button. Turn off and disconnect the machine as the cycle is ending. Place the dough in a 4-quart oil-sprayed plastic container. Refrigerate the dough for 12 to 24 hours, covered.
- Inside a large mixing dish, combine almond paste, sugar, almond extract, egg white, and crushed cinnamon to make the marzipan filling. Beat using an electric mixer until smooth. Place aside.
- Using parchment paper, line a baking sheet. Form a 12-by-20-inch rectangle out of the refrigerated dough on a floured surface. Spread the almond filling onto the dough, leave a one-inch border along the edges. Top with chopped almonds. Form the dough into a 20-inch log. Roll the log on a sugared surface to coat it in raw sugar. Roll the log between your palms to extend it to 30 inches. Form it into a circle on the baking pan, resembling a pretzel. Allow it to rise for 45 minutes, covered loosely using a clean tea towel.
- About 20 minutes before baking, let the oven preheat to 375°F (190°C).
- With a brush, coat the sugar-coated dough with the beaten egg white glaze and top with chopped almonds. Bake the bread for 25 to 30 minutes or until golden brown and firm to the touch. After baking, take the bread out of the pan and let it cool thoroughly on a wire rack before serving.

PREP. TIME: 20 MINUTES | COOK TIME: 1 HOUR 50 MINUTES

LOAF:1 LB. 4|1,5 LBS. 6| 2 LBS. 8

PER SERVING: CALORIES 174 | TOTAL FAT 15G | PROTEIN 6G | CARBS 35G

Ingredient		1 Lb.	1.5 Lbs.	2 Lbs.
For the dough:				
o	Dried porcini mushrooms	0.5 ounce	0.75 ounce	1 ounce
o	Boiling water	7/8 cup	1⅝ cups	1¾ cups
o	Yeast	2/3 tablespoon	1 tablespoon	1⅓ tablespoons
o	All-purpose flour	1⅓ cups	3 cups	4 cups
o	Whole wheat flour	2/3 cup	1.5 cups	2 cups
o	Buckwheat flour	1⅓ tablespoons	3 tablespoons	4 tablespoons
o	Cornmeal	3 tablespoons + 1 teaspoons	1/4 cup + 2 tablespoons	1/3 cup
o	Salt	1 teaspoon	2¼ teaspoons	1½ tablespoons
o	Sugar	2/3 tablespoon	1 tablespoon	1⅓ tablespoons
o	Coarsely ground black pepper	2/3 teaspoon	1 teaspoon	1⅓ teaspoons
o	Porcini oil	1/4 cup + 1 tablespoon	5/16 cup	1/3 cup
o	Caraway seeds	2/3 tablespoon	1 tablespoon	1⅓ tablespoons
To finish the focaccia:				
o	Porcini Oil	1⅓ tablespoons	2 tablespoons	2⅔ tablespoons
o	Coarse Salt	1⅓ teaspoons	2 teaspoons	2⅔ teaspoons

Directions:

- Add the mushrooms to a small bowl and submerge in boiling water until very tender or for around 10 to 15 minutes.
- Drain the liquid using a fine-mesh sieve over a glass 2-cup measure, gently pressing the mushrooms to get out as much extra liquid as possible. Keep the liquid aside.
- In the machine, combine all of the dough ingredients and 1 cup of the reserved mushroom juice, select Dough or Manual, and push Start.
- Roll the dough into a 9-inch round and set it on a baking sheet or pizza pan, lightly sprinkled using cornmeal when ending the final kneading.
- Cover using a clean tea towel and set it aside in a warm location to rise until nearly doubled in volume. Because buckwheat and whole wheat flour contain very little gluten, it will take around an hour.
- Let the oven preheat to 425°F and place the rack in the middle. Make little indentations on the top of the dough using your fingertips.
- Drizzle the oil on the top and season with salt. Bake for 20 to 25 minutes, or till the top is golden brown and the underside is dry and toasted. Serve immediately or at room temperature.

Note: *Always remember to observe the dough's consistency. If it's too dry, you can add a bit more of the mushroom juice or water. If it's too wet, sprinkle in a bit more flour. It's essential to maintain the right consistency for proper bread texture and rise.*

11.7. Rustic Pizza Bread

PREP. TIME: 20 MINUTES | COOKING: 1 HOUR 50 MINUTES

LOAF: 1 LB. 4 | 1,5 LBS. 6 | 2 LBS. 8

PER SERVING: CALORIES 310 | TOTAL FAT 11G | PROTEIN 8G | CARBS 44G

Ingredient	1 Lb.	1.5 Lbs.	2 Lbs.
o *Olive oil*	1 tablespoon	1.5 tablespoons	2 tablespoons
o *Raw honey*	1 tablespoon	1.5 tablespoons	2 tablespoons
o *Fine sea salt*	2/3 teaspoon	1 teaspoon	1 teaspoon
o *Wheat flour (+ extra for dusting)*	1 ⅔ cups	2 ½ cups	3 ¼ cups
o *Vital wheat gluten*	2/3 tablespoon	1 tablespoon	1⅓ tablespoons
o *Instant yeast*	1 ⅓ teaspoons	2 teaspoons	2 ½ teaspoons
o *Garlic powder*	1 teaspoon	1 ½ teaspoons	1 ½ teaspoons
o *Partitioned dried oregano*	1 ⅓ tablespoons	2 tablespoons	2 tablespoons
o *Sundried tomatoes, chopped*	1/3 cup	2/5 cup	½ cup
o *Black chopped olives, pitted*	1/3 cup	2/5 cup	½ cup
o *Part-skim mozzarella cheese, shredded*	½ cup	⅔ cup	¾ cup
o *Beaten egg white*	(Adjust to coat)	(Adjust to coat)	(Adjust to coat)
o *Sesame seeds*	1 ⅓ teaspoons	2 teaspoons	2 teaspoons

Directions:

- Follow the manufacturer's instructions when adding 1 1/4 cups of oil, water, honey, salt, gluten, flour, garlic powder, yeast, and 1 tablespoon of oregano to a bread machine.
- Program the bread maker to make "dough." Move the dough to the floured work surface after it has finished the dough-making process.
- The rectangle dough is roughly 10-12 inches broad and long, depending on the bread maker. Sprinkle the dough liberally with the remaining oregano, olives, tomatoes, and mozzarella.
- Roll the dough into a log shape, jelly-roll style, beginning on one of the short sides. Remove the paddle from the bread machine's baking pan and place the dough log in the pan, ensuring the seam is on the bottom. Return the pan to the bread maker and let the loaf rise for 1 hour.
- Once the bread has risen, brush the top gently using a white egg and sprinkle with sesame seeds. Set the bread machine to "Bake-only" mode for 1 hour and 20 minutes.
- Check the bread after 1 hour. Bread is ready when it is somewhat browned on top and has a hollow appearance.
- Remove from the pan immediately and set aside to cool before slicing. Cooled bread can be kept refrigerated or at room temperature for 2 to 3 days if well-wrapped in plastic.

CHAPTER 12: BREAD MACHINE JAM RECIPES

12.1. Fresh Apricot Jam

PREP TIME: 15 MINUTES | COOK TIME: 1 HOUR

SERVE 2½ CUPS.

PER SERVING: CALORIES 60 | TOTAL FAT 1G | PROTEIN 1G | CARBS 10G

Ingredient	**For 1 Lb./1,5lbs./2 Lbs.**
o *Fresh apricots, pitted and chopped*	2 cups
o *Fresh lemon juice*	1 tablespoon
o *Powdered fruit pectin*	½ box (2 ounces / 57 g)
o *Sugar (or to taste)*	1¼ cups
o *Powdered fruit pectin*	½ box (2 ounces / 57 g)

Directions:

- In a bread machine pan, combine the apricots and lemon juice. Pectin should be sprinkled on top. Allow for a 10-minute resting period. Pour in the sugar.
- Select the Jam cycle in the machine and hit the Start button. At the end of the cycle make sure to wear kitchen gloves so as not to burn yourself and, carefully remove the pan. Immediately afterwards pour the jam with rubber spatulas into jars; they should be heat-resistant.
- Allow to cool for a short time.
- Storage options include freezing the jam in freezer bags or keeping it in the refrigerator for up to six weeks.

Note: The ingredient quantities are calculated to be suitable for most bread machines, regardless of size. If you have a particularly small bread machine, it's recommended to check its maximum capacity before proceeding. The quantities are appropriate for small, medium, and large machines.

PREP TIME: 15 MINUTES | COOK TIME: 1 HOUR

SERVE 2½ CUPS.

PER SERVING: CALORIES 60 | TOTAL FAT 1G | PROTEIN 1G | CARBS 10G

Ingredient	For 1 Lb./1,5lbs./2 Lbs.
o *Salt*	Pinch
o *Sugar (as needed)*	1 cup
o *Fresh lemon juice*	1 tablespoon
o **Pitted fresh Bing cherries*	1 pound (454 g)
o *Powdered fruit pectin*	1½ tablespoons

*After pitting, you will get whole cherries & bits

Directions:

- In a bread pan, add the salt, cherries, lemon juice & sugar. Allow about 15 minutes to allow the sugar to fully dissolve. Pectin should be sprinkled on top.
- Select the Jam cycle in the machine and hit the Start button. At the end of the cycle make sure to wear kitchen gloves so as not to burn yourself and, carefully remove the pan. Immediately afterwards pour the jam with rubber spatulas into jars; they should be heat-resistant.
- Allow to cool for a short time.
- Storage options include freezing the jam in freezer bags or keeping it in the refrigerator for up to two months.

Note: The ingredient quantities are calculated to be suitable for most bread machines, regardless of size. If you have a particularly small bread machine, it's recommended to check its maximum capacity before proceeding. The quantities are appropriate for small, medium, and large machines.

PREP TIME: 15 MINUTES | COOK TIME: 1 HOUR

SERVE 2½ CUPS.

PER SERVING: CALORIES 60 | TOTAL FAT 1G | PROTEIN 1G | CARBS 10G

Ingredient	**For 1 Lb./1,5lbs./2 Lbs.**
○ *Sugar (or to taste)*	1½ cups
○ *Fresh blueberries, rinsed*	1 pound (454 g)
○ *Crème de cassis liqueur*	3 tablespoons
○ *Powdered fruit pectin*	½ (2-ounces / 57-g) box
○ *Fresh lemon juice*	2 tablespoons

Directions:

- In the bread pan, combine all of the ingredients. Allow about 15 minutes for the sugar to fully dissolve.
- Select the Jam cycle in the machine and hit the Start button. At the end of the cycle make sure to wear kitchen gloves so as not to burn yourself and, carefully remove the pan. Immediately afterwards pour the jam with rubber spatulas into jars; they should be heat-resistant.
- Allow to cool for a short time.
- Storage options include freezing the jam in freezer bags or keeping it in the refrigerator for up to two months.

Note: The ingredient quantities are calculated to be suitable for most bread machines, regardless of size. If you have a particularly small bread machine, it's recommended to check its maximum capacity before proceeding. The quantities are appropriate for small, medium, and large machines.

PREP TIME: 15 MINUTES | COOK TIME: 1 HOUR

SERVE 2½ CUPS.

PER SERVING: CALORIES 60 | TOTAL FAT 1G | PROTEIN 0.5G | CARBS 9G

Ingredient	For 1 Lb./1,5lbs./2 Lbs.
o *Fresh lemon juice*	2 tablespoons
o *Sugar (or to taste)*	1 cup
o *Large peaches*	3 to 4 (about 1 pound / 454 g)
o *Powdered fruit pectin*	1 (2-ounce / 57-g) box

Directions:

- Peaches should be peeled and pitted. Crush coarsely in a food processor by pulsing a few times or with a potato masher. It will give you approximately 2 1/2 cups.
- In a bread pan, combine the peaches, sugar, and lemon juice. Allow about 30 minutes for the sugar to fully dissolve. Pectin should be sprinkled on top.
- Select the Jam cycle in the machine and hit the Start button. At the end of the cycle make sure to wear kitchen gloves so as not to burn yourself and, carefully remove the pan. Immediately afterwards pour the jam with rubber spatulas into jars; they should be heat-resistant.
- Allow to cool for a short time.
- Storage options include freezing the jam in freezer bags or keeping it in the refrigerator for up to two months.

Note: The ingredient quantities are calculated to be suitable for most bread machines, regardless of size. If you have a particularly small bread machine, it's recommended to check its maximum capacity before proceeding. The quantities are appropriate for small, medium, and large machines.

PREP TIME: 15 MINUTES | COOK TIME: 1 HOUR

SERVE 2½ CUPS.

PER SERVING: CALORIES 60 | TOTAL FAT 1G | PROTEIN 0.5G | CARBS 9G

Ingredient	For 1 Lb./1,5lbs./2 Lbs.
o *Sugar*	2 1/2 cups
o *Julienned Lemon Zest*	3 tbsps.
o *Fresh Lemon Juice*	4½ tbsps.
o *Fruit Pectin (Powdered)*	2 tbsps.
o **Large Kiwis*	6-7 (approx. 1.6 pounds / 725 g)

* *Peeled, sliced, and coarsely chopped*

Directions:

- In the bread pan, combine all the ingredients. Allow about 20 minutes for the sugar to fully dissolve.
- Select Jam cycle on the machine and hit the Start button. At the end of the cycle make sure to wear kitchen gloves so as not to burn yourself and, carefully remove the pan. Immediately afterwards pour the jam into jars they should be heat-resistant, help yourself by utilizing a rubber spatula.
- Allow to cool for a short time.
- Storage options include freezing the jam in freezer bags or keeping it in the refrigerator for up to two months.

Note: The ingredient quantities are calculated to be suitable for most bread machines, regardless of size. If you have a particularly small bread machine, it's recommended to check its maximum capacity before proceeding. The quantities are appropriate for small, medium, and large machines.

Hello dear reader,

Using a bread machine isn't just about following recipes. It's a true art, and like any art, there's always something new to learn and perfect.

First Bonus: To aid you on this journey, I've crafted a **special advanced guide** for you. This guide isn't just about more recipes—it's about elevating your skills. Dive into advanced techniques, learn to adapt using alternative ingredients, and discover how to get the most out of every feature of your bread machine. Whether it's lactose-free breads, vegan treats, yogurts, cheeses, sauces, and more, this guide has got you covered.

Second Bonus: But wait, there's more! Within the pages of this advanced guide, you'll find a **special surprise**, exclusively designed to reward your passion for cooking and inquisitiveness.

Ready to dive in? Download your bonuses now using the link provided or by scanning the QR code below and elevate your culinary journey!

Link: https://bit.ly/459mh2P

SCAN ME

Thank you for choosing "Bread Machine Cookbook". Happy reading and bon appétit!

MEASUREMENT CONVERSION CHART

CUPS	OUNCES	MILLILITERS	TABLESPOONS
8 cups	64 oz.	1895 ml	128
6 cups	48 oz.	1420 ml	96
5 cups	40 oz.	1180 ml	80
4 cups	32 oz.	960 ml	64
2 cups	16 oz.	480 ml	32
1 cup	8 oz.	240 ml	16
3/4 cup	6 oz.	177 ml	12
2/3 cup	5 oz.	158 ml	11
1/2 cup	4 oz.	118 ml	8
3/8 cup	3 oz.	90 ml	6
1/3 cup	2.5 oz.	79 ml	5.5
1/4 cup	2 oz.	59 ml	4
1/8 cup	1 oz.	30 ml	3
1/16 cup	1/2 oz.	15 ml	1

CONCLUSION

Thank you for making it to the end of this book. Bread is one of the most fundamental foodstuffs required for human survival. Everyone eats bread differently, depending on what they like best. Bread is also noticed to be the most desired meal item. Even though there are regional differences in how bread is made, the fundamental components are the same everywhere: wheat, yeast, oil, water, salt, sugar, milk, and eggs.

Bread is a staple at every meal of the day, from breakfast to dinner, because it goes with just about anything you might eat. It is also used to celebrate significant occasions or when someone has accomplished or achieved a certain objective.

Making bread at home is a simple task. Wheat flour, yeast, salt, and oil are the only mandatory ingredients; sugar, milk, butter, and eggs are optional but greatly improve the flavor and texture. Then, you'll need your bread machine and a dry, clean surface to knead the dough on. If you own a business, a bread machine will save you a ton of money and time by eliminating the need for as many workers to knead the dough you feed it. As a result, it saves money.

You have found ample beloved bread recipes in this book for you to pick from. Hopefully, you've also discovered your favorite recipes, those that you enjoy and will continue to make whenever you get the chance. Now that you've seen how simple it is to make fantastic and perfect bread with our bread machine, you're free to experiment and let your imagination run wild.

Good luck!

Printed in Great Britain
by Amazon

47471894R00073